# PAPAL ERROR

# Papal Error?

## A Defense of Popes Said to have Erred in Faith

ST. ROBERT BELLARMINE, S.J.

Doctor of the Church

Translated by
Ryan Grant

MEDIATRIX PRESS

MMXV

ISBN:069256599

Translated from:
*De Controversiis Fidei Christianae*
Ingolstadt, 1588

# TABLE OF CONTENTS

# INTRODUCTION

HIS little work is an excerpt from Bellarmine's larger treatise *On the Roman Pontiff*, book 4, which follows after the assertion of what was already universally taught at that time, but not completely understood nor decreed by the Church's solemn magisterium, that the Pope was infallible in his teaching on faith and morals when teaching the whole Church. These chapters then, being 8-14 of that work, follow to test and prove this claim historically, wherein he posits exculpatory evidence against claims that 40 Popes had grievously erred in matters of faith. It should be noted that we have renumbered these chapters in this work accordingly.

Much as with the doctrine of Papal infallibility itself, St. Robert Bellarmine does not endeavor to show the impeccability of Popes, rather that in matters of faith, where the Popes are actually authoritative, they did not err. Some matters treated here are the objection of certain Protestants, while others are even of Catholics who are confused on the decrees or behavior of these Popes.

A word must be said about the validity of some of the history contained herein. St. Robert Bellarmine makes arguments based on historical evidence and testimony. The principles of his

i

historiography are not foreign to our own day, the sources closer to the event are more likely to be correct than those later, agreement of writers makes for a strong witness in the matter and consistency of documents is necessary for determining their truth.

Another vehicle St. Robert uses is text criticism, done at a period when that science was in its infancy. In this he shows himself rather astute, albeit he was limited to the resources of his own time. Scholarship has moved on since the 16$^{th}$ century and removed attributions to various authors with it. Some documents he references were held as valid by all men of that time, but in fact are thought today by scholars of the ancient period to be forgeries, such as the "Pontifical of Pope Damasus" which is the basis for the crime of Pope Marcellinus related in the first chapter, which likewise is thought today to be a myth by Church historians. What is important for us, is that not only did St. Robert Bellarmine believe it, but so also did his contemporaries.

There are also some assertions where Bellarmine was not followed by the subsequent tradition, such as his assertion that during the Pontificate of Pope Liberius, he was no longer held to be Pope and instead Felix II was created Pope in his place. We have preserved Bellarmine's account in full, regardless of whether one would that something were changed or altered. It is also important that we remember that Bellarmine was a theologian, and while a very great one, is but a private doctor in those matters where there is no consensus of the whole tradition, let alone a judgement of the magisterium.

Lastly, as a sort of preamble to the work, it is worth noting that these chapters were used as a blueprint at Vatican I by the fathers of that Council to further scrutinize these cases and be sure of the limits and nature of papal authority. Bellarmine thus lays out four basic propositions; Two of these Catholics must believe with divine faith per the subsequent decree of Vatican I (which were no less incumbent upon the believer in Bellarmine's time, though then they were so by the universal teaching of all theologians), namely that the Pope is infallible when judging matters of Faith and Morals and defining these as matters that must be believed by all the faithful. This particular distinction is important, for the Pope, outside of this very narrow category, does not enjoy infallibility, thus in private letters, private teaching, their acts, behavior, etc., Popes can give scandal, they can give opinions that are in fact false, but they cannot teach the whole Church and bind it to believe error.

The next two propositions follow (though they are not laid out in this order in the original): a) that the particular Roman Church can never err; b) that the Pontiff as a particular person cannot be a heretic. Concerning the first, Bellarmine brings strong arguments from the Fathers in regard to the Roman Church. That argument is that the Roman Church as such, while it may have members that are in error, cannot become apostate because its Bishop is the Pope. This would seem to follow from the eloquent patristic testimony given to the Roman Church. Then, there the last proposition, which Bellarmine phrases thus:

"It is probable and may piously be believed that not only as 'Pope' can the Supreme Pontiff not err, but he cannot be a heretic even as a particular person by *pertinaciously* believing something false against the faith." This must be born in mind as one of the criterions Bellarmine is attempting to defend throughout this treatise, and for him it is inseparable from the Pope's power in faith and morals, and the indefectibility of the Roman Church. He continues:

"It is proved: 1) because it seems to require the sweet disposition of the providence of God. For, the Pope not only should not, but cannot preach heresy, but rather should always preach the truth. He will certainly do that, since the Lord commanded him to confirm his brethren, and for that reason added: 'I have prayed for thee, that thy faith shall not fail,' that is, that at least the preaching of the true faith shall not fail in thy throne. How, I ask, will a heretical Pope confirm the brethren in faith and always preach the true faith? Certainly God can wrench the confession of the true faith out of the heart of a heretic just as he placed the words in the mouth of Balaam's ass. Still, this will be a great violence, and not in keeping with the providence of God that sweetly disposes all things.

"2) It is proved *ab eventu*. For to this point no [Pontiff] has been a heretic, or certainly it cannot be proven that any of them were heretics; therefore it is a sign that such a thing cannot be." (*On the Roman Pontiff*, book 4, ch. 6.)

Thus we hasten to Bellarmine's treatment of the historical cases.

# CHAPTER I

*On the Errors Which are Falsely Ascribed to the
Roman Pontiffs Peter, Linus, Anacletus, Thelesphorus,
Victor, Zephyrinus, Urban, Pontian, Cornelius and
Marcelinus, Who Were not only Popes, but even
Martyrs*

ET us now come to the individual Popes whom our adversaries contend have erred. The first is Peter. Nilos Cabásilas, in his book, *On the Primacy of the Roman Pontiff,* writes that Peter erred not only once but twice concerning faith. Further, he even supposes that by this argumentation he has proven that the Roman Pontiffs can err in faith. Certainly no Roman Pontiff received greater privileges from God than Peter. Moreover, it is clear from Scripture that Peter erred twice, both when he denied Christ,[1] and when he compelled the Gentiles to Judaize.[2] The Lutheran Centuriators of Magdeburg add, apart from these two errors, another thirteen falls of St. Peter, on which we wrote elsewhere.[3]

---

[1] Matthew 26:69-75.

[2] Galatians 2:11-14.

[3] Cent. 2, lib. 2, ch. 10, col. 558, 559, 560. (See: *On the Roman Pontiff,* book 1, ch. 28).

We respond: When St. Peter denied Christ, he had not yet begun to be the Supreme Pontiff, for it is certain that ecclesiastical rule was handed to him by Christ in the last chapter of John, since the Lord said to him after the resurrection: "Simon, son of John, feed my sheep." Therefore, that denial of Peter cannot be numbered among errors of the Roman Pontiffs. Besides, I add that Peter denied Christ with words, but not truly in his heart; hence Peter did not throw off the confession of faith, nor faith itself, as we showed previously.

Now, on the other hand, when St. Peter compelled the Gentiles to Judaize, this was not an error of preaching but of conduct, as Tertullian suggests in his work *de Praescriptionibus adversus haereticos*. St. Peter did not ratify by some decree that they must Judaize; rather, he formally taught the contrary in Acts XV. Nevertheless, when he was still in Antioch, he separated himself from the dinner table of the Gentiles lest he would give offense to those recently converted to the faith from the Jews, and by his example compelled them to Judaize in a certain measure, even Barnabas. But we do not deny that Popes can offer the occasion of erring through their own bad example; rather, we deny that they can prescribe the whole Church to follow some error *ex cathedra*. Moreover, the examples and doctrines of the Pontiffs are not equally pernicious to the Church, seeing that the

Lord instructed them, saying: "Do what they say, but do not do what they do."[4]

The second is Linus, who immediately succeeded St. Peter in the pontifical seat. He is mocked by the Centuriators because he had forbidden women to go into church without their heads covered.[5] He said: "It is established that no woman (certainly worthy of episcopal care) should enter into the Church with her head uncovered." But what if Linus would have added, that it were not fitting on account of the angels? Without a doubt they would claim that it is superstition. But the Centuriators have forgotten, I believe, that the Apostle Paul did not judge it unworthy of his care to command that women should veil their head on account of the angels;[6] St. Ambrose explains that this custom must be especially preserved in the Church on account of the reverence of priests, who are called "angels" in the Scripture.

The third is Anacletus, whom the Centuriators condemn in the same book,[7] because he built a memorial of St. Peter and adorned it. Certainly St. Peter merited so little from the Church that it was fitting for his memory to altogether cease! But if blessed Anacletus must be blamed because he established some monument for the bones of St.

---

[4] Matth. 23:3.

[5] Cent. 1, lib. 2, ch. 10, colum. 627.

[6] 1 Corin. 11: 6-10.

[7] lib. 2, cap 20, col. 628.

Peter, how much greater, I ask, was the sin of Constantine the Great, who built such a sumptuous basilica and adorned it with so many golden and silver gifts to the memory of St. Peter? But otherwise concerning all these things, all pious men judge differently than our adversaries judge them now. Certainly the very noble writer Gaius, so near to apostolic times, as Eusebius relates,[8] calls the tombs of Peter and Paul the trophies of the Apostles, by which the Roman Church is fortified as if by the firmest columns.

John Chrysostom expressed his supreme desire of coming to Rome so that he could fall prostrate at the tombs of Peter and Paul.[9] And I ask that you listen to the great honor with which he speaks about the city of Rome as well as the bodies and tombs of the Apostles: "Just as a great and strong body has two bright eyes, (Rome) has the bodies of those saints. Heaven does not so glitter, when the sun sends forth its rays; just as the city of the Romans pouring forth the light from those two lamps throughout the world. ... How great are those two crowns that adorn the city? What golden chains encompass her about? What fonts does she have? This is why I celebrate this city, not because of its supply of gold, nor its many columns, nor on account of another fancy, but on account of those columns of the Church. Who will grant me now to

---

[8] lib. 2 hist. ch. 25.

[9] In homily 32 on the Epistle to the Romans.

throw myself around the body of Paul? To be fastened to his tomb? To see the dust of that body?" He further adds: "This body fortifies the city, which is more secure than innumerable towers, walls and ramparts; and with it is also the body of Peter. For Paul also honored him while he was alive, saying: 'I went up to see Peter.'"

Moreover, Theodoret not only praises Rome for many things, but most especially for the tombs of the Apostles, which he says illuminate the souls of the faithful. I pass over many other testimonies that can be added since they are proper to the disputation on the relics of the saints, which will be taken up in another place.

The fourth is Thelesphorus, who was the ninth Pope after St. Peter, and ended in a glorious martyrdom, as Irenaeus witnessed.[10] The Centuriators accuse him in these words: "He first commanded clerics that they should fast from meat for seven weeks before Easter, although it is against what is written: 'Let no man judge you in regard to food and drink.' Next, he increased the Masses and augmented their rites, and also bound it to the seasons, although the Lord's supper was not established on account of number, or ceremonies, or time. Likewise, he raised the dignity of clerics and their sanctity exceedingly above the people, as if it were not written that all are one in Christ Jesus. Moreover, he would not have priests charged or

---

[10] lib. 3, ca. 3.

accused by the people, and he calls that law the firmest wall of his order, constituted by himself and the Fathers against persecutors."[11]

These clearly are the errors of Thelesphorus, which are judged to be errors by the Centuriators because such are against the rule of Luther; but if we judge justly, would it not rather more be said that the dogmas of Luther, which do not suffer the choice of foods, nor Masses, nor the rank of priests above the people, are erroneous and false, because they disagree with the rule of Thelesphorus? For since Thelesphorus was a saint and a martyr, and very close to the times of the Apostles, and even could have spoken with Peter, Paul and John, is it not more believable that he could better recognize the doctrine of Christ than Luther, who was not a martyr and lived 1400 years after the times of the Apostles? These are petty arguments of the Centuriators, and answered a thousand times.

For what they advance from Paul: "Let no man judge you on food and drink," are not opposed to taking up abstinence from meat, or having such abstinence appointed to a season to subdue the wantonness of the body; rather they are opposed to those who never use certain foods for the very reason that they were unclean according to the Old Law. Thus the same citation of Paul applies to them: "Let no man judge you in food or drink, or on the

---

[11] Cent. 2, cap. 10, col. 212.

6

day of the feast, or a new moon, or the Sabbath, which are shadows of things to come."[12]

They add that the Lord's Supper was not established in regard to number, nor in regard to rite or time; we do not deny this. But what happens from there? Did Telesphorous err on that account, when he wished three Masses to be celebrated on Christmas, and added other rites, and established the times in which Masses were to be celebrated? For although the Lord's supper was not established in regard to number, rite and time, still the number, rite and time ought to be determined in regard to celebrating the very supper of the Lord rightly, unless perhaps order would be less fitting to such a Sacrament than disorder.

Next, they add from the Apostle: "All of you are one in Christ Jesus."[13] This proves nothing less than that priests are no more worthy than laity. Paul explains precisely how we are all one in Christ when he says we are one body, where there are various members, eyes, hands, feet, and some are more noble and worthy than others.[14]

The fifth is Pope Victor, the fifteenth Pope from St. Peter. He was once infamously accused by certain heretics, as though he had taught that Christ was only a man, as Eusebius relates.[15] Yet, Eusebius

---

[12] Coloss. 2: 16.

[13] Galat. 3: 28.

[14] Rom. 12:4-8; 1 Cor. 12:4-31.

[15] Lib. 5, hist. ch. 28.

proves this was a false calumny in the same place; it
is certain that the prince of that heresy, Theodotus,
was excommunicated by Victor.

The sixth is Pope Zephyrinus, the successor to
Pope Victor, who seems to have ratified the heresy
of the Montanists. Tertullian writes in his book
against Praxea, that the Roman Pontiff, recognizing
the prophecies of Montanus, advanced the peace to
the churches of Asia and Phrygia by that
recognition and was persuaded by Praxea to recall
the letters of peace which he had already sent out. It
is certain from the histories that Zephyrinus was
the bishop of Rome at that time. For that reason,
Rhenanus, in his annotations to Tertullian, placed
this remark in the margin, that the bishop of Rome
accepted Montanism. Nor can it be said that in this
period this heresy was not yet condemned by the
Church, since, as Tertullian says in the same place,
Praxeas persuaded the Pope to recall the letters of
peace, for the very reason that his predecessors had
already condemned that heresy.

I respond: Trust is not to be altogether placed in
Tertullian on this question, as he was a Montanist
himself at this time. Just as a little earlier Artemon
had falsely claimed that Victor, the Roman Pope,
agreed with him (which we have already shown
from Eusebius), so at this time when Tertullian was
a Montanist he tried to drag the Roman Pope into
the opinion of Montanus. Otherwise, why did
neither Eusebius, nor anyone else, record this error
in the Roman Pontiff?

Still, because often it is the case that lies are founded upon some truth, it is believable that Pope Zephyrinus was persuaded by the Montanists that the doctrine of Montanus was not different from the doctrine of the Roman Church, and therefore, the same Pope wished to restore peace to them which his predecessors had taken away. He did not even approve the error which his predecessors condemned; rather, he thought the Montanists were falsely accused concerning these errors. This is not, however, to err concerning faith nor to accept the error of Montanism, as Rhenanus pretends, but to err in his person, which happens also to many other holy men. Ruffinus writes in his book that Arius, so that he might persuade the Emperor Constantine that he was Catholic, wrote his belief by a careful artifice so that he should be reckoned as a Catholic, yet still be recognized for what he was by his own followers.[16] Moreover, Pope Leo I warns that bishop in no uncertain terms to command the Pelagians returning to the Church to abjure heresy, because most of the time they deceive the Church with a confession of their faith that is so composed that they might appear Catholic, when they are not.[17] This very thing appears to have also happened to Pope Zephyrinus.

The seventh is Urban, the eighteenth Pope from St. Peter. The Centuriators condemn him in these

---

[16]   Lib. 10, hist. ch. 11.

[17]   Epist. 86 to Nicetas of Aquileia.

words: "He established Confirmation after Baptism, but blasphemously says, through the imposition of the hands of bishops Christians receive the Holy Spirit and become fully Christian."[18] They also condemn Pope Cornelius for the same error.[19]

Yet, in the first place, they are lying when they say the Sacrament of Confirmation was established by Pope Urban. For its use exists in the Acts of the Apostles 8 and 19, where the Apostles impose their hands over the baptized, so that they would receive the Holy Spirit. And besides, Tertullian, who is older than both Urban and Cornelius, mentions Confirmation in many places. In his work, *de Resurrectione Carnis*, he says: "Flesh is washed, so that the soul will be without stain; the flesh is anointed, that the soul be consecrated." And in *de Praescriptiones contra Haereticos*, speaking about the Devil, who imitates our Baptism and Confirmation: "He imbues, at any rate, certain believers and his faithful; he signs his soldiers there on the forehead." And in *de Baptismo*: "Furthermore, going out from the laver we are anointed with blessed Unction." And a little further: "Next the hand is imposed, calling forth through blessing and inviting the Holy Spirit." Do you not see with Tertullian Unction, a sign on the forehead, imposition of hands, arrival of the Holy Spirit? Therefore, what could Urban establish? It is certain that Tertullian was older than

---

[18] Cent. 3, ch. 10, col. 277.

[19] Ibid, col. 282.

Urban. For Tertullian lived in the times of the Emperor Severus, and his son Antoninus, as the Centuriators teach basing themselves on Jerome in the same volume of the *Centuries*.[20] What of the fact that the same Centuriators number among "the blemishes of Tertullian" that he recognized anointing after Baptism as well as the necessary sign of the Cross? Therefore, how can they embrace this idea that Confirmation was established by Urban, when they already placed it among the "blemishes of Tertullian," who is older than Urban?

Next, when the Centuriators add that what Urban says is a blasphemy, namely that men receive the Holy Spirit and are made fully Christians through the imposition of hands of bishops, they do not require refutation, since they advance no proof. Especially when Cornelius also says the same thing, as they affirm, and even Cyprian,[21] Cyril,[22] Augustine[23] and other Fathers frequently do.

The Eighth Pope who is said to have erred is Pontianus, the successor of Urban. The Centuriators accuse him of writing that priests confect the body of the Lord by their own mouth, and give it to the people, and that God receives the sacrifices of others as well as forgives their sins and reconciles

---

[20] Cent. 3, ch. 10, col. 277.

[21] lib. 1, epistle 12.

[22] Catechesis 3, mystagogica.

[23] *in epistolam Ioannis*, tract 6.

11

them through the priests.[24] The Centuriators so greatly call this teaching a blasphemy, but they advance nothing whereby they prove it is a blasphemy. They ought not take it so badly if we believe a holy martyr and what was established by the Apostles more than what was established by Luther, especially since we read the same thing in the writings of all the ancient Fathers.

Listen to Jerome in his epistle to Heliodorus: "Far be it that I would speak evil about anyone who, succeeding to the apostolic step, confects the body of Christ with his own holy mouth, through whom we are also Christians; who, having the keys of the kingdom of heaven, in a certain measure, judge before the day of judgment."

Listen to Augustine, where he speaks about captive women among the barbarians: "Pray to God for them, and entreat that he would teach them to say such things as St. Azarias poured forth to God in his prayer and confessions among other things. They are thus in the land of their captivity, just as they [the Israelites] were in that land, where they could not sacrifice to the Lord in their custom; just as they cannot offer oblation at the altar of God, or discover there a priest, through whom they might offer it to God."[25]

Listen to Chrysostom, in the third book on priesthood, where he says: "To purge the leprosy of

---

[24] Cent. 3, ch. 10, col. 278.

[25] Epist. 122 ad Victorianum.

the body, or that I might speak more truly, not even to purge, but to show one has been purged, it was lawful to do so to the priests of the Jews alone. On the other hand, to our priests, I do not say to prove they have been cleansed, but that it has indeed been conceded to them to cleanse not the leprosy of the body, but the filth of the soul." Therefore, when Pontianus says that through the priests the body of the Lord is confected, the offerings of others are received by God and the sins of men are forgiven, he says what even the most approved authors said, Jerome, Augustine, Chrysostom, and still all the rest, whom I pass over for the sake of brevity.

The ninth is Pope Cornelius, whom the Centuriators claim taught that only water was to be offered in the chalice of the Lord.[26] Such an error was shown to be against the Gospel, but this is a very impudent calumny. They prove this only from what Cyprian relates to Cornelius where he makes many arguments against this error.[27] But Cyprian does not say this is Cornelius' error, but that of others. Next, that epistle was not written to Cornelius, but to Caecilius, a certain African bishop, as other examples show. But the Centuriators then by chance drank more liberally and with sparkling and heavy eyes read one for another. Add that Pope Alexander, the predecessor of Cornelius, already published a decree lest anyone would offer

---

[26] Cent. 3, ch. 6, col. 145 and ch. 7, col. 165.

[27] Lib. 2, epist. 3, ad Cornelium.

anything other than wine mixed with water in the chalice of the Lord.

Next, if from this epistle they condemn others, why do the Centuriators not condemn themselves? Accordingly, Cyprian, more often in this epistle, calls the Eucharist a sacrifice, and does not teach that only water or only wine must be offered, but water mixed with wine. The Lutherans, however, obstinately deny that the Eucharist is a sacrifice and judge that only wine must be consecrated in the chalice without water.

The tenth is Pope Marcelinus, who sacrificed to idols, as is certain from the Pontifical of Damasus, the Council of Sinvessanus, and from the epistle of Nicholas I to the Emperor Michael. But Marcelinus neither taught something against faith, nor was a heretic, or unfaithful, except by an external act on account of the fear of death. Now, whether he fell from the pontificate due to that external act or not, little is related; later he abdicated the pontificate and shortly thereafter was crowned with martyrdom. Still, I believe that he would not have fallen from the pontificate *ipso facto*, because it was certain to all that he sacrificed to idols only out of fear.

# CHAPTER II

## On Liberius and Felix II

HE eleventh Pope who is accused of error is Liberius. Now, although the Centuriators do not dare to define anything on Liberius,[1] still, Tilman Hesh boldly affirms that he was infected with the Arian heresy.[2] And, of course, he has serious authors as witnesses for his opinion; St. Athanasius,[3] St. Jerome and Pope St. Damasus.[4]

I respond. There are two things certain concerning Liberius, and one in doubt. Firstly, it is certain that from the beginning of his pontificate even to exile, he suffered for the Catholic faith and was a keen defender of the Catholic religion. All writers who spoke on those times witness this fact, such as Ammianus Marcelinus, Athanasius in both *Apologies*; Ruffinus, Sulpitius Socrates, Sozomen, Theodoret, and Nicephorus.[5]

Secondly, it is certain that Liberius, after he returned from exile, was also truly orthodox and pious. As the Church historian Socrates writes, after

---

[1] Centur. 4, ch. 10, colum 1284.

[2] De Ecclesia, lib. 1 cap. 9.

[3] Epist. ad solitariam vitam agentes.

[4] Chronicus et Catalogus scriptorium; in Fortunatiano; *In vita Liberii.*

[5] Marcellinus, Historiae suae, lib. 15; Ruffinus, Hist. lib. 10 cap. 22; Socrates, Sacrae Historiae, lib. 2.; Sozomen, Hist. Ecclesiastic., lib. 2, cap. 29. Thedoret, Lib. 4 cap 10. Lib. 2, ch. 16 and 17.; Necephorus, Lib. 9 ch. 35, 36, and 37.

15

he returned from exile, Liberius refused to receive the Macedonians into the Church unless they would openly lay aside heresy.[6] Besides, after his death, he was held as a saint, as is clear from the words of St. Ambrose: "It is time, sister, to return to the precepts of Liberius, of holy memory, that the holier the man, the more pleasing conversation should approach."[7] Likewise, we see in the words of Epiphanius that: "Eustathius lead a legation to blessed Liberius, the bishop or Rome, together with many bishops."[8] Basil also says in epistle 74 to the western bishops: "Certain things were proposed to us by the most holy Liberius."

Next, Siricius, who was the third [Pope] after Liberius, declared in an epistle to Hymericus that Liberius was his predecessor of revered memory. How I ask, could these Fathers call Liberius most blessed after his death, if he had died in heresy? Therefore, only one doubt remains: whether in the middle period, that is, in the very return from exile, he did something against the faith. And certainly, Sulpitius, Socrates, Sozomenus and Nicephorus show in the citations we have noted, that Liberius was always the same and never diminished in the constancy of the faith. On the other hand, Athanasius and Jerome obviously say the opposite; that being tired of exile he at length bent and

---

[6] Lib. 4, ca 11.

[7] De Virginibus, lib. 3, in principio.

[8] Haeres. 75.

subscribed to heresy. To which it can be added St. Hilary, who says against the Emperor Constantius: "You turned your war even to Rome, you snatched from there the bishop, and you are so miserable that I do not know whether you banished a man with greater impiety than you sent him back."[9] Ruffinus, however, affirms that he could not discover for certain whether Liberius had subscribed to heresy.[10]

From such opinions there seems to us to be a second truer one. For Athanasius, Hilary and Jerome are both more ancient and important than the rest, and they relate the matter not as dubious but rather as certain and investigated. Besides, epistles written in the hand of Liberius can be read from the Vatican Library, which were written partly to the Emperor, and partly to the Oriental bishops; therein he sufficiently showed that he would acquiesce to the will of the Emperor. To this, unless we should affirm that Liberius at some time defected from the constancy that must be guarded in the faith, we are compelled to exclude Felix II, who managed the pontificate while Liberius was alive, from the number of the Pontiffs, although still, this very Felix was venerated by the Catholic Church as a Pope and martyr. Next, Sozomen[11] and Nicephorus[12] hint more obscurely that Liberius, in

---

[9] Adversus Constantium.

[10] Hist., lib. 10, ch. 27.

[11] Hist., lib. 4, ch. 14.

[12] Lib. 9, ch. 37.

the Council of Sirmium, agreed with Valens and Ursacius (the Arians) and made peace with them, received back his see, aided even by letters of the same council. But although they would have these matters thus, still Liberius neither taught heresy nor was a heretic, but only sinned by an external act, just as St. Marcellinus, and, unless I am mistaken, he sinned less than Marcellinus.

St. Athanasius teaches that he was not truly a heretic,[13] when he says that Liberius was compelled against his will by the force of the rack to do what he did. Nor must it be though to be truly his opinion which had been twisted from him by threats and terrors, especially given what he advanced when he was freely disposed; that he did not teach heresy can easily be proved. It is gathered from the words of Athanasius as well as from the epistles of Liberius himself, that Liberius committed two faults: 1) That he subscribed to the condemnation of Athanasius; 2) That he had communicated with heretics; but in neither did he expressly violate the faith. For although heretics persecuted Athanasius for the faith, nevertheless, they pretended it was not due to the faith but morals, and Liberius consented to the condemnation of Athanasius on that basis, not on account of the faith. For equal reason he communicated with heretics, because they feigned that they were Catholics. In his epistles, Liberius

---

[13] Loc. cit.

says that he communicated with Oriental bishops because he discovered that their faith agreed with the Catholic faith, and was foreign to the Arian treachery.

Besides, Sozomen and Nicephorus[14] say that in the peace which Liberius made with the Arian bishops, nothing was demanded from him except that he would subscribe to the Confession of Sirmium published against Photius and the Confession of Antioch published in Enceniis. These confessions also do not have the word ὁμοούιος; still they are Catholic, and Hilary, in his book on councils, shows that they are Catholic. It happens that Liberius not only did not subscribe to the Arian confession, but even published a *Confession* before he left from Sirmium wherein he excommunicated those who denied that the Son is the same as the Father in substance, as well as in all other matters, as Nicephorus and Sozomen relate in the works we have cited. The reason he did this is because the Arians spread a false rumor that Liberius began to teach that the Son is not consubstantial with the Father.

Now someone will say: If that is so, then why does Jerome say that Liberius bent and subscribed to heresy in the end? I respond: Although Liberius did not expressly consent to heresy, still he was interpreted as having done so since he permitted Athanasius to be condemned, whom he knew

---

[14] Sozomen, Lib. 4, ch. 14.; Nicephorus, Lib. 9 ch. 37.

suffered persecution for the sake of the faith, and communicated with Ursacius and Valens whom he knew were heretics although they feigned otherwise. Therefore, this is what Jerome meant.

The twelfth who is accused of error in faith by the heretics is Felix II, whom Tilman Hesh contends was an Arian[15] and attempts to show it from the testimony of St. Jerome, who in the catalogue of writers, on Acacius, says thus: "Acacius, whom they named μονόφθαλμου (monophthalmou) because he had one eye, was the bishop of Caesarea in Palestine. Under Constantius the Emperor he became famous because the Arian bishops constituted him Felix at Rome in place of Liberius." But we respond that Felix was never an Arian, although he communicated with the Arians in the time in which he was not the true Pope. Still, when he began to be a true Pope, not only was he not an Arian but he even publicly detested the Arians, and on account of their persecution he received the crown of martyrdom from the Lord.

Therefore, it must be explained as briefly as it can be done, the history of the pontificate of Liberius and Felix, from which a marvelous providence of God will appear in the Apostolic see. After Liberius departed into exile on account of the Catholic Faith, the Roman Clergy swore never to admit another man as Pope while Liberius lived. Jerome witnesses that in his *Chronicle*, although his

---

[15] De Ecclesia, lib. 1 ch. 9.

words have been transposed. These words "Who, being in exile, all the clergy swore, etc.," which are placed in the year 351 ought to be placed after these: "Liberius, the bishop of the Romans, is sent into exile," which are placed in the year 361.

Next, by a work of the Arians, and especially of Acacius, the bishop of Caesarea, Felix a Roman deacon was created a bishop in place of Liberius; on account of this good deed he freely communicated with him although he was not an Arian. Thus Ruffinus writes: "In Liberius' place, Felix his deacon was substituted by the heretics and he was not tainted by diversity of sect, but agreement of communion and ordination."[16] Theodoret says: "Liberius was succeeded by a faithful deacon named Felix, who, although he preserved the whole faith expressed in the Council of Nicaea, still he freely communicated with those who labored to subvert the same. And for that reason no one living at Rome wished to enter the Church if he was inside."[17]

Sozomen also writes the same thing.[18] Jerome does not disagree in his catalogue of writers on Acacius; for that term [Arian] is added to the name of Felix, and it seems to have crept in from somewhere else. Accordingly, the ancient manuscript codices do not have that term, as Marianus Victorius remarked on this place, nor

---

[16] Hist., lib. 10, cap. 22.

[17] Hist., lib. 2, cap. 17.

[18] Hist., lib. 4 ch. 10.

does the translation into Greek made by St. Sophronius have it. Now what I find most important is that Freculph[19] and Ado of Vienna,[20] when referring to the whole sentence in this citation of Jerome, do not have the term "Arian".

Next, it is not at all credible that Jerome and Ruffinus could have such a discrepancy in their history, that one would deny something and the other affirms it. Even if Felix were an Arian (which still to this point is not proven) he did no harm to the Apostolic see. At that time Felix was an anti-pope, not a true and legitimate Pope, as two cannot be Pope together. The true Pope was still alive, namely Liberius. Wherefore (as we related from Theodoret above) no Catholic in Rome wanted to communicate with Felix at that time.

Next, two years after the fall of Liberius, concerning which we spoke above, then the Roman clergy abrogated Liberius from the pontifical dignity and conferred it upon Felix, whom they knew to be Catholic. From that time Felix began to be a true Pope. Although Liberius was not a heretic, still it was considered that, on account of the peace made with the Arians, that he was a heretic, and from that presumption his pontificate could rightly be abrogated. For men cannot be held to thoroughly search hearts; yet when they see one who is a heretic by his external works, then they judge

---

[19] Lib. 4, ch. 80.
[20] in Chronico.

simply and condemn him as a heretic. Jerome shows this in his *Chronicle*, when he says that many from the Roman clergy perjured themselves and went to Felix. They are said to have perjured themselves, because they did not keep the oath that they had taken to not receive another Pontiff.

Next, Felix, now a true Pope, noticing the danger to the Church and the faith, without a doubt inspired by God who did not desert his Church, not only receded from communication with the Arians, but even compelled a council and declared the Emperor Constantius, as well as the bishops Ursacius and Valens with whom Liberius had made peace, to be truly heretics. And for that reason, when Liberius returned to the city, Felix was ejected with his own by the Arians, and died not long after, whether beheaded, or consumed in labors. That is not known for certain. This, however, bears on the matter, that Felix, after the fall of Liberius, was a true Pope, and died for the Catholic faith, which is proved by these arguments.

First, Damasus (or whoever is the author of the *Pontifical*), clearly witnesses  the life of Felix. St. Jerome appears to mean the same in the *Chronicle*, when he says on the Roman clergy: "After a year with Felix they were thrown out, because Liberius, conquered by the exhaustion of exile and subscribing to a heretical depravity, entered Rome as a victor." These words mean persecution moved against Felix, and it was moved by those who

23

favored the Arians. From that it follows that Felix himself suffered persecution for the Catholic faith.

Secondly, all ancient Martyrologies, both those lain down by Bede, Ado and Usuard, and even the manuscripts for the fourth day before the Kalends of August (29 July), place the memory of St. Felix II, Pope and Martyr, who declared Constantius a heretic. Add that St. Gregory I, both in his antiphonary and in his Sacramentary, places the whole ecclesiastical office that must be read for Mass in the day of St. Felix, Pope and martyr, on this same day, the fourth before the Kalends of August. Moreover, this Felix was a Roman Pontiff, and hence, the one about whom we are speaking, as Micrologus witnesses.[21] Therefore, since the Catholic Church has venerated this Felix for a thousand years as a Pope and martyr, he ought not be excluded from the number of Pontiffs, even if we could advance no other reason.

Thirdly, Pope Felix, the grandfather of St. Gregory, is called Felix IV by very ancient writers, such as by John the Deacon[22] and by Leo Hostiensis.[23] But he could not be fourth, unless the Felix about whom we are writing would have been the second. There were no more than two Felixes, apart from this our Felix, before the fourth. Therefore, a thousand years ago this Felix was held

---

[21] Lib. Ecclesiast., observationum, cap. 43.

[22] De vita B. Gregorii, lib. 1, ch. 1.

[23] Chronici Cassiensis, lib. 1, ca. 1.

in the number of Pontiffs, and they did not make him in the number of the schismatics.

Fourthly, when there was some ambiguity in Rome in the year 1572 whether this St. Felix ought to be placed in the new Martyrology a marble box was discovered in the Basilica of Sts. Cosmas and Damian, with this inscription in the marble in ancient characters: "HIC IACET CORPVS SANCTI FELICIS PAPÆ, ET MARTYRIS, QUI CONSTANTIVM HÆRETICVM DAMNAVIT."[24]

At any rate, after the death of St. Felix, Liberius again reconciled the Roman clergy to himself, and was an outstanding Catholic prelate, as we showed above from the history of Socrates on the case of the Macedonians. For that reason in the consensus of all he began to sit legitimately again, and sat even to death. This is the reason why in the catalogue of Popes, some of the Fathers like Augustine[25] and Optatus,[26] could not place Felix, because clearly, the whole time of Felix was rolled into the pontificate of Liberius.

The thirteenth is a certain Pope (anti-Pope) Leo, whom several say succeeded Felix II and was plainly Arian; he died by the same type of death in which Arius perished, namely by the effusion of all his intestines, while at the toilet. Vincentius relates

---

[24] Here lies the body of St. Felix, Pope and Martyr, who condemned Constantius as a heretic.

[25] Epist. 165.

[26] Lib. 2.

this,[27] as well as Conrad Halberstatensis in his Chronicle. The Centuriators do not reckon this improbable.[28]

There is no doubt that this Leo was an anti-pope. It is certain that Leo I was the one who sat in the time of the Council of Chalcedon; this is, around a hundred years after the times of Felix II. Next, all ancient writers, such as Jerome, Augustine, Optatus, Theodoret, Ruffinus, and still more recent writers, like Sigebert, Martin Polanus, Platina and everyone else, place Damasus after the death of Liberius and Felix.

Perhaps this false story arose from the imagined opinion of the heresy of Liberius, and the persecution against Catholics after Felix II was expelled. After the expulsion of Felix, leisurely men falsely reckoned that Liberius began to take on the nature of a fierce lion against Catholics and imagined an Arian Pope Leo sat after Felix II.[29] But these are numbered among the fables.

---

[27] Speculi histoiralis, lib. 15, ch. 23.

[28] Cent. 4, ch. 10, in vita Felicis II.

[29] Translator's note: To be clear, not only historians but even the Church has not followed Bellarmine's judgment on Felix II. On the one hand Bellarmine brings credible arguments; still it muddies the waters even more. Modern historians know that the 2nd formulary of Sirmium, which Liberius signed, was not in itself heretical but could be interpreted as such.

# CHAPTER III

*On Siricius, Innocent and Seven Other Popes*

THE fourteenth Pope is Siricius, whom John Calvin accuses of error because in his letter to the Spanish he calls the union of spouses pollution.[1] But Calvin impudently lies, which is his custom. For Siricius did not appeal to the pollution of true and legitimate spouses; rather, their illicit unions where, union after carrying out a public penance again returned to the same union, on account of which they had done penance. No one ever did penance for a legitimate marriage.

The fifteenth is Pope Innocent I, whom the Centuriators,[2] in the life of Innocent, say gravely erred because he had commanded that a consecrated virgin, already veiled, who will have married or committed fornication, was not to be received to Penance while the man with whom she had sinned was alive.[3] It seems wicked, they say, that a woman doing penance ought not be absolved, unless first the one who seduced her should die. Likewise, in epistle 18, he wrote to Antiochenus at Alexandria that the baptisms of Arians were certainly valid, but that the Holy Ghost was not conferred through them, because they are separated from the Church. There, it seems, he would have it

---

[1] Institutes, lib. 4, ch. 12 §24.

[2] Epist.2, cap.12.

[3] Cent. 5, cap. 10.

that the efficacy of holy baptism depends on the goodness of the minister, which is against the common doctrine of the Church. Moreover, he taught[4] that a man cannot be a priest who receives a widow as a wife, since the law of Moses commanded in Leviticus that a priest should receive a virgin as a wife, as if Christians were still held to the judicial laws of the Old Testament.

I respond: Firstly, Innocent wished to say that virgins should not be received in Penance who refused to be separated from the adulterer, except after his death, and this is most just. Those who persevere in their sins ought not be absolved by the Church.

I speak now to the second point. Innocent speaks in that place about those who were baptized or ordained by heretics, when they were polluted by the same heresy. Those of this sort receive the Sacrament of baptism, or of ordination, but they do not receive the grace of the Holy Spirit, which cannot be present in heretics. And in ordination, not only do those ordained by heretics not receive grace, but they do not have the right to exercise Orders. The ordaining bishop loses that right through heresy, nor can he give what he does not have.[5]

Now I address the third argument. Innocent did mean that we are bound by the laws of the Jews;

---

[4] Epistle 22, ch. 1.

[5] See the Glossa, 1, quaest. 1, can. Arianos.

rather he wished to argue from a similar thing, or rather more, from a better thing in this mode. Priests in the Old Testament were held by divine precept not to marry a widow. Therefore, it is much more fitting that in the priesthood of the new law, the Church should require that they be not husbands of widows, on account of the excellence of Christian priesthood.

The sixteenth is Celestine I, whom Lorenzo Valla asserts was infected with the Nestorian heresy, in his *declamatione de falsa donatione Constantini.* But what Laurence says is false, since not only was it never recorded that Celestine was infected with this heresy, but he is the one who especially condemned that heresy, which is clear from Prosper of Aquitaine[6] as well as from the whole Council of Ephesus. Valla was deceived by the equivocation of the name. For there was a Celestine that was a Pelagian heretic who held certain things in common with the Nestorians.

The seventeenth is St. Leo I, who said that those women who think that their husbands are dead, or because they never return from captivity, marry another, do not sin; still, if the first should return, they are held to renew the first marriage. If however, the men do not wish to do so, they are not bound.[7] Here there are two errors: 1) That a woman would not sin if she married another man when she

---

[6] Chronicum anni CCCXXXI.

[7] Epist. 79 ad Nicetum.

thinks the first husband is alive but simply never returned; 2)That a woman can remain with the second husband if the first refuses her. The Centuriators have much to say about this error.[8]

I respond: in neither case did Leo err. For when he says that a woman who marries would not sin while the prior husband is still alive, he spoke only on a woman who will marry because she supposes that the first husband is dead, and he eloquently explained the same thing. He said, in regard to a woman who will marry because she thinks her husband is never going to return, not that she sins nor that she does not, because he thought the matter was known in itself, for without a doubt she sins. However, when he says a woman ought to return to the first husband, if he wishes it, consequently he wishes to be understood that a man ought to return to the woman, if she wills him, even if otherwise he does not want her. Husband and wife are equal in this matter. Therefore, if one of the spouses should wish to return to wedlock, the other is necessarily bound to obey: if, however, neither wishes to return, they can remain separated, in regard to the use of marriage, and this alone is what St. Leo permitted. From that it does not follow that a woman can remain with the second husband, for the same Leo clearly says in the same place that the first marriage is indissoluble, and necessarily

---

[8] Cent. 5, ch. 10, in vita Leonis I.

must be reformed, while the second may be dissolved because it could not be a true marriage.

The eighteenth is Pope Gelasius. The Centuriators note that he has two opinions, which are erroneous according to Catholics.[9] One is in the book against Eutychus, where he says that true bread remains with the flesh of Christ in the Sacrament. The second we discover with Gratian that one cannot consume one part of the Sacrament of the Eucharist while not the other without great sacrilege.[10] Thus, either Gelasius erred in these two, or we err who teach and follow the contrary.

I respond to the first: That book is not of Pope Gelasius. It is either of Gennadius, who wrote a book of the same title to Pope Gelasius, or of Gelasius Caesar, the bishop, whom Jerome calls to mind near the end of this *Catalogue of Ecclesiastical Writers.* Accordingly, Pope Gelasius wrote five volumes against Eutychus, as Trithemius relates; but this one, however, is only one scanty book. Next, this author promises that he is going to gather the teachings of almost all the Fathers, on the Incarnation of the Lord, and when he adds fifteen Greek Fathers he only advances two Latin authors, Ambrose and Damasus. Yet he omits Cyprian, Hilary, Jerome, Augustine, Innocent, Leo, Prosper, and the like, whom Pope Gelasius never omitted; nay more, nor did any Latin author do so.

---

[9] Cent. 5, ch. 4, de coena Domini; cap. 10 in vita Gelasii.

[10] De consecrate., dist. 2, canon.

Therefore, it seems manifest that this author was Greek and not Latin. To the second, I say that Gelasius speaks in that canon only on the priest offering the sacrifice, who cannot take only one species without sacrilege, because he would render an imperfect sacrifice.

The nineteenth is Pope Anastasius II, who is accused of three errors. Firstly, because he communicated with Photinus, who had communicated with the heretic Acacius without a council of bishops, priests and clergy of the whole Church. Secondly, because he wanted to secretly recall Acacius, whom Felix and Pope Gelasius had condemned. Thirdly, because he approved baptism and orders confirmed by the same Acacius; on account of such errors and sins the same Anastasius, after a divinely constituted plague had set in, immediately died. Not only does the author of the *Pontificalis* write these things in the life of this Anastasius, whose account Tilman Hesh followed,[11] but even Gratian,[12] and the Centuriators.[13]

I respond: It is quite false that Anastasius wished to recall Acacius. This is certain from Evagrius[14] and from Nicephorus[15] as well as

---

[11] De Ecclesia lib. 1, cap. 9.

[12] Can. Anastasius, dist. 19.

[13] Cent. 6, cap. 10, in vita Anastasii.

[14] Lib. 3, cap. 23.

[15] Lib. 15 and 17.

Liberatus. Acacius died in the time of Pope Felix, from whom Anastasius was third. How, therefore, did Anastasius wish to recall someone to his see who had long been dead? But, some would say, he at least wished to restore his name. On the other hand, an epistle of this Pope Anastasius is extant, sent to the emperor by the same name, in which he asks the Emperor to command the name of Acacius be held in silence in the Church, seeing that he had been most justly condemned by his predecessor Pope Felix. What Gratian says, namely, that Anastasius erred in this epistle because he wanted the Sacraments of baptism and order which Acacius had conferred to be held as valid,[16] does not show Anastasius a heretic, but Gratian inexperienced. Who does not know that Catholics that are baptized by heretics are truly baptized, and likewise those who are ordained by them are truly ordained, even when the ordaining bishop was a heretic and remained so, at least in regard to the [Sacramental] character?

Now, that part on Photinus is probably a lie, just as the revocation of Acacius, but even if it were true, would Anastasius not be Catholic for that reason? Or is it not lawful for the Supreme Pontiff to absolve one excommunicated without a council of all bishops, priests, and clerics of the whole Church? Now the matter which they add, that Pope Anastasius immediately died by a heaven sent

---

[16] Canon. Ita Dominus, distinction 19.

plague, seems to arise for the reason that the heretical emperor Anastasius died from being struck by lightning at the same time, as the historians relate in his life.[17] Otherwise it is without doubt a fable.

The twentieth Pope is Vigilius. Liberatus relates in chapter 22 of his *Breviary* that Vigilius wrote an epistle to Theodora the Empress and other heretics, whereby he confirmed their heresy and declared anathema on those who confessed that there are two natures in Christ.

I respond: Many reckon that heretics corrupted this citation of Liberatus, for the reason that it seems contrary to what is said in the *Pontifical*. But since no vestige of corruption appears in the book of Liberatus, and really, the relation is not opposed to that of the *Pontifical*, another response must be given. Therefore, I say that Vigilius wrote that epistle, and condemned the Catholic faith, at least from exterior profession, but this does nothing to obstruct our case. For he did that when Pope Sylverius was still living and at that time Vigilius was not Pope, but an anti-Pope. For two men cannot be true Popes at the same time, and it was certain then to all that Sylverius was the true Pope, although he abided in exile.

It must be known, that Anthemius, the heretic, was deposed from the Episcopate of Constantinople by Pope Agapetus. Then the empress [Theodora]

---

[17] Bede, Cedrenus, Zonaras and Paul the Deacon.

sought from Sylverius, the successor of Agapetus, that he would restore Anthemius. Yet when he refused, Vigilius, then an archdeacon, promised the empress that he would restore Anthemius, if he could be made Roman Pontiff: immediately, by the command of the empress, Belisarius, his general, expelled Saint Sylverius from his own see and sent him into exile, and created Vigilius Pope, or, rather, an antipope. In that period it would be no marvel if he erred in faith, and could even plainly be a heretic. Still, he did not even define something against the faith as Pope, nor was he a heretic in spirit. Accordingly, he wrote that nefarious epistle, and it was unworthy of a Christian man; still, he did not openly condemn the Catholic faith in it, nor manifest a heretical spirit, but secretly, on account of the lust for control, just as Liberatus says in the aforementioned citation, which also appears from the epistle of Vigilius himself. He writes that they should be careful lest anyone should see that epistle, and that all should be secret for a time. Vigilius then was upon the very narrow straights that his ambition had thrown him. For if he openly professed heresy, he would fear the Romans, who were never seen to suffer a heretic to sit in the chair of Peter; if, on the other hand, he would profess the Catholic faith, he feared the heretical Empress, whose work had secured for him the pontificate. Therefore, he devised the plan that he would be a Catholic at Rome, and meanwhile through, his letters feign that he was a heretic to the emperor.

# PAPAL ERROR

It happened a little afterward, that Sylverius died and Vigilius, who to that point sat in schism, now began to be the sole and legitimate Pontiff for certain through the confirmation and reception by the clergy and the Roman people.

From this time neither error nor feigning of error was discovered in Vigilius, but rather, supreme constancy in the faith even to death, as it shall appear. For he received with the pontificate the strength of faith and he was changed from a weak chaff into the most solid rock. When the Empress Theodora, having relied upon the secret letters as well as the promise of Vigilius, asked from him that he would restore the aforementioned Patriarch Anthemius, as he had promised, he wrote back that he had promised rashly and gravely sinned in that promise. Therefore, he could not nor would fulfill what he had promised, lest he would add sins to sins. For that reason, when the Empress became angry, he was sent into exile, and miserably tortured even to death. That much is not only written in the *Pontifical*, but Paul the Deacon also annotated it in the *Life of Justinian*, as well as Aimonius.[18] Even the Centuriators themselves,[19] as well as the same Liberatus who was cited earlier, say that Vigilius was later miserably afflicted by the adherents of  that very heresy which he had secretly fostered in the beginning.

---

[18] De gestis Francorum lib.. 2, ch. 32.

[19] Cent. 6, cap. 10, in vita Vigilii.

Next, Vigilius, after the death of Sylverius, was a true and holy Pontiff, as all witness who lived in those times and wrote something on him. Pope Gregory I says: "The memory of Pope Vigilius must be recalled, constituted in the royal city, who promulgated the sentence of condemnation against Theodora, then the empress."[20] Cassiodorus says: "It is certain that Origen was condemned at that time by Blessed Pope Vigilius."[21] Arator wrote a preface to the Apostolic Acts, which he dedicated to Pope Vigilius, and begins thus: "To the holy, most blessed, Apostolic, Pope Vigilius, first of all priests in the whole world." Next, it is certain from Evagrius that the Fifth General Council was confirmed by Vigilius, in which that heresy that Theodora favored and which the adversaries of Vigilius accused him of adhering to, was condemned.[22]

It could be said that the epistle of Vigilius, which Liberatus calls to mind, was fabricated by heretics. Liberatus, moreover, may have believed false rumors that the heretics had spread. That the heretics fabricated a certain epistle in the name of Pope Vigilius to Theodora and Justinian can be recognized by certain indications in the Sixth Council, action 14; but whatever the case on this, it

---

[20] Lib. 2, epist. 36 ad Episcopos Hyberniae.

[21] Lib. de divinis lectionibus, cap. 1.

[22] Lib. 4, cap. 37.

is enough for us that when he was a true Pope, he made no error in faith.

The twenty-first is St. Gregory I. Durandus accused him of error because in an epistle[23] he permitted priests to confer the Sacrament of Confirmation, which is fitting for bishops alone to confer by divine law. On account of this citation of Gregory, Adrian asserts that the Pope can err in defining dogmas of faith.[24]

I respond: Firstly, it is not St. Gregory, but rather Durandus and Adrian who have erred. The Council of Florence, in the *Instructione Armenorum*, and the Council of Trent, in the last canon of its 7th Session, teach that the ordinary minister of Confirmation is the bishop. Wherein it follows that extraordinarily, even a non-bishop can be the minister of this Sacrament. Next, Gregory did not publish some decree on the matter, but only conceded to certain priests, that in the absence of the bishops, they may confirm. Hence, if Gregory erred in this matter, it was not of doctrine but an error of example or fact. There is another error which is attributed to St. Gregory but falsely, and we will speak on it below when we treat on Gregory III.

The twenty-second is Boniface V, whom the Centuriators grievously condemn[25] because he

---

[23] Lib. 3, epistle 26 to John the bishop of Caralitanum.

[24] In quaest. De Confirmatione, last article.

[25] Cent. 7, ca. 10.

taught that Christ redeemed us only from original sin.[26] I respond: The Centuriators added that term *only* on their own. For Boniface says: "Therefore, hasten to acknowledge him, who created you, who breathed the breath of life into you, who sent his only-begotten son for your redemption, so that he would deliver you from original sin." The reason why he did not call to mind other sins is because original sin is the principal one, and it was for the purpose of destroying it that Christ principally died. Wherefore, in John I we read: "Behold the Lamb of God, behold he who takes away the sins of the world. In Greek: "Τὴν ἁμαρτιαν τοῦ κόσμου" that is, the sin of the world; this is original sin, because it alone is common to the whole world. For many have no other sin, such as all children.

---

[26] Epistle to King Edwin of England, c.f. Bede, lib. 2, Hist. Anglorum, cap. 10.

# CHAPTER IV
## On Honorius I

HE TWENTY-THIRD is Honorius I. Nilos Cabásilas contends that he was a Monothelite heretic in his book on the primacy of the Roman Pontiff. The Centuriators assert the same thing and place him among manifest heretics.[1] Not just heretics, but even several Catholics contend Honorius was a heretic, such as Melchior Cano.[2] There are six arguments that they bring to the fore.

1) From the epistles of Honorius himself, for there are extant two epistles of Honorius to Servius; one in the Sixth Council, action 12, the other the same, act 13. Furthermore, they say that in each Honorius approves the doctrine of Servius, the leader of the Monothelites, and bids it not to be said, that Christ had two wills, or operations [*operationes*].

2) From the Sixth Council, act 13, where Honorius was condemned as a heretic and his letters were burned, and in the following acts the condemnation was repeated by all.

3) From the Seventh Council, last act, where the whole Council declared anathema to Honorius, Sergius, Cyril and the other Monothelites, and

---

[1] Cent. 7, cap. 10 in vita ipsius, and cap. 11, col. 553.

[2] De Locis, lib. 6, last chapter.

repeated the same in an epistle which it wrote to all clerics.

4) From the Eighth Council, act 7, where the letter of the Roman Council under Pope Adrian II was read and approved. In that letter the Pope asserts with the Council that Honorius was judged after his death by the Sixth Council, because he had been accused of heresy.

5) From the epistle of Pope Agatho, who in a letter to the Emperor Constantius (which is contained in the $4^{th}$ act of the Sixth Council), he declares Anathema to Honorius, just as to the Monothelites.

6) From Leo II, who in an epistle to the same emperor, which is contained at the end of the council, the same Honorius is cursed; just as one who had contaminated the Apostolic See with heresy.

7) From various Greek and Latin writers who witness that Honorius was a heretic. Thrasius, the bishop of Constantinople, asserts this, in an epistle to the Patriarchs, which is contained in act. 3 of the Seventh Council. Likewise Epiphanius, a Catholic deacon, in a disputation with a heretic named Gregory, which is contained in act 6 of the Seventh Council, volume 2. Psellus relates it in a poem about the Seventh Council, as does Bede,[3] and it is in the *Liber Pontificalis* concerning the life of Leo II.

---

[3] De Sex Ætatibus; in vita Constantini IV Imperatoris.

41

Yet several wrote on behalf of Honorius: Albert Pighius,[4] Cardinal Hosius[5] and Onufrius in an annotation to Platina in the life of Honorius. Their reasoning is much more efficacious than of the other side, as will be clear in the answers to the arguments.

To the first: I respond in two ways. It is possible that these two epistles were fabricated and inserted into the general council by heretics. Certainly one should not say this rashly, yet in this matter it is certain that in the Fifth Council heretics inserted fictitious epistles of the Roman Pope Vigilius, as well as Mennas, the Patriarch of Constantinople. That was detected in the Sixth Council,[6] while the acts of the Fifth Council were re-read. They discovered three or four groups of things inserted and placed in these epistles by heretics. What wonder would it be if they carried out the same plans in the Sixth Council?

To the second I say, no error is contained in these epistles of Honorius. For Honorius confesses in these epistles what pertains to the matter of two wills and operations in Christ, and he only forbids the name of one or two wills, which then were unheard of, and he did it with prudent counsel. That he confessed the matter itself is clear from the

---

[4] Hierarchiae Ecclesiasticae, lib. 4 cap. 8.

[5] Contra Brentium et Joannes a Lovanio, lib. 2; in de perpetua cathedrae Petri protectione et firmitate, lib. 2 ch. 11.

[6] Actione 12 et 14.

words of the second epistle: "We ought to confess both natures in the one Christ, joined in a natural unity, working in harmony with the other, and also confess operations. And certainly the divine operation, which is of God, and the human operation, which is of God, carrying it out not in division, nor confusion, informing the other but not changing the nature of God into man, nor the human into God, but confessing the different natures whole, etc." This confession is very Catholic, and altogether destroys the Monothelite heresy.

Moreover it can be shown that Honorius acted with great prudence when he forbade the names of one or two operations. For then it was the beginning of this heresy, and nothing on these terms was yet defined by the Church. Then, Cyrus of Alexandria began first to preach one operation in Christ, while conversely Sophronius of Jerusalem opposed himself to Cyrus, preaching two operations in Christ. Cyrus related this contention both to Sergius of Constantinople and to Honorius of Rome. Therefore, Honorius, fearing that which later would happen, wanted to conciliate each opinion, and at the same time abolish the matter of scandal and contention from sight. He acted to prevent this contention from becoming a serious schism, and at the same time he saw the faith would be preserved without these terms. Therefore, he wrote in the first epistle that they ought to abstain from the term "one operation," lest we would seem to place one nature in Christ with the followers of Eutychus, and again from the term of two operations, lest we seem to place two persons in Christ with Nestorius. "Let no one, being offended by the term 'of two operations' think by some madness that we agree with the Nestorian sects, or certainly if again we sensed that one operation must be affirmed, that we would be reckoned by itching ears to confess the foolish madness of the Monophysites."

In the second epistle, while teaching the manner of speaking and reconciling the opinions: "Therefore, bearing the scandal of a novel invention, it is not fitting for us to preach defining one or two operations; but for one which they mean by 'operation,' it is fitting for us to confess there is one operator, Christ the Lord, truthfully in each nature; and for two operations, after the term of twin operations has been removed, or rather more of two natures, that is, of divinity and flesh taken in one person of the only begotten Son of God the Father unconfusedly, indivisibly, and also inconvertibly to preach his proper workers with us." Certainly, this can only be praised.

Then they say, however, that a little below he clearly preaches only one will in these words: "Wherefore, we profess one will of our Lord Jesus Christ." I respond: In that place, Honorius spoke only on the human nature, and meant that in the man, Christ, there were not two wills opposing each other, one of the flesh and the other of the spirit; but only one, namely the spirit. For the flesh in Christ desired absolutely nothing against reason. Moreover, this is the mind of Honorius, and that is plain from the reason that he gave. Thus he says: "Wherefore, we affirm one will of our Lord Jesus Christ, because certainly our nature was assumed by the divinity there is no fault, certainly that which had created sin, not that which was damaged after sin." This reasoning is null, if it is advanced to prove in Christ, God and man, there is only one will; it is very efficacious if thence it must be proved that in Christ the man there were not contrary wills of the flesh and spirit. That contrariety is born from sin, but Christ has a human nature without sin.

Next, because someone could have objected with the citations of the Gospel, "I have not come to do my will," and "Not what I will, but what you will," where Christ seems, as a man, to have contrary wills, indeed one wicked, whereby it wished not to suffer; and the other good, whereby it did not wish to fulfill the first will, but the contrary which was conformed to the will of God. Honorius responds a little later: "It is written, 'I have not come to do my will, but the will of Him who sent me,' and 'Not what I will, but what you will Father' and other things of this sort. They are not of a different will, but taken up from the dispensation of humanity. This was said on account of us, to whom he gave an example, in order that we might follow in his footsteps, the pious teacher imbuing his students, that each one of us should not do his own will, but rather more that he would prefer the will of the Lord in all things." In other words, Christ did not have contrary wills, so that it would be fitting for him to conquer and mortify one. Instead he so spoke as if he had contrary wills, that he would teach us to mortify our own will, which often strives to rebel against God.

St. Maximus, who lived in the time of Honorius, confirms this with serious testimony. He wrote a dialogue against Pyrrhus, the successor of Sergius, which is still in the Vatican Library. In that *Dialogue* he introduces Pyrrhus the heretic, advancing in front of him the testimony of Honorius, then he responds that Honorius was always Catholic, and proves it with another source, from the testimony of the secretary of Honorius himself, who wrote those epistles dictated by Honorius, and who was then still living, and said that. Moreover the Secretary witnesses the mind of Honorius was never to deny two wills in Christ, and whenever it seems to deny two wills, it must be understood on two contrary and opposed wills in the same human nature, which is discovered in us from sin, but was not in Christ. St. Maximus records these very words:

PYRRHUS: What do you have whereby you could respond about Honorius, who wrote in his letters to Sergius in previous times that he clearly professed one will in our Lord Jesus Christ?

46

## CH. IV: ON POPE HONORIUS I

MAXIMUS: I reverence each of these letters, and a more certain interpretation must be given. Did not his scribe, who wrote those epistles in the name of Honorius, who still lives, say that he adorned the West with the splendor of every virtue and discipline in religion; or the citizens of Constantinople, who will have nothing but what is pleasing to them?

PYRRHUS: I reverence what he wrote.

MAXIMUS: But he [the secretary] wrote to Emperor Constantius about that epistle, at the command of Pope John, saying "We rightly said one will of our Lord Jesus Christ, it must not be taken up as if it spoke on two wills of divine and human nature, but only of one in human nature." Since Sergius wrote to preach that there were two particular contrary wills of Christ, we wrote back that Christ did not have two contrary wills.

Furthermore, in the whole epistle, Honorius contends it must not be said that in Christ as God and man there is one or two wills, how did he so forget himself that he would then clearly affirm one will? Therefore, he did not say there is one for God and man, but one for Christ as man alone, as the words which follow and the secretary witness. Therefore, we hold that there is no error in these epistles.

I say to the second: without a doubt, the name of Honorius was inserted among those who are

47

condemned by the Sixth Council by rivals of the
Roman Church, and likewise whatever else is said
against him. I prove this, a) because Anastasius the
Librarian witnesses this in his history drawn from
Theophanus the Isaurian, a Greek; and b) it was
nearly an ordinary custom of the Greeks to corrupt
books. For (as we said) in the Sixth Council itself,
act 12 and 14, many corruptions were discovered
made by heretics in the Fifth Council. And Pope
Leo[7] sought from the Greeks why they had
corrupted his epistle to Flavian even though he was
still living? Pope Gregory asserted that at
Constantinople they had corrupted the Council of
Chalcedon, and he suspected the same about
Ephesus.[8] And he adds that the codices of the
Romans by far had greater veracity than those of
the Greeks: "Because the Romans, just as they do
not have frauds, so also they do not have
impostures."

Next, Nicholas I, in his epistle to Michael,
referring the emperor to the epistle of Adrian I,
said: "If still, it has not been falsified in the hands of
the church of Constantinople from the custom of
the Greeks, but is just as it was sent from the
Apostolic See, so far it will have been preserved."
He did not say this without cause, for the things he
alleges in the epistle to Photius from the epistle of
Adrian to Tharasius, are not contained in that

---

[7] Epist. 83 ad Palaestinos.

[8] Lib. 5, epist. 14 ad Narsem.

epistle, as it is read in the Seventh Council. Therefore the Greeks cut out that citation, because it took action against the honor of Tharasius. Therefore, if the Greeks corrupted the Third, Fourth, Fifth and Seventh Council, would anyone be surprised if they had corrupted the Sixth also? Especially since it is certain that a little after the Sixth Council concluded, many bishops again went up to Constantinople and published the canons in Trullo; the purpose of the said bishops seems to have been nothing other than to revile and condemn the Roman Church.

Thirdly, the council could not condemn Honorius as a heretic, unless it opposed the epistle of St. Agatho, nay, more even itself; plainly it asserts the contrary. For Pope Agatho in Epistle I to the Emperor, which was read in that very council (sess. 4), says: "This is the rule of the true faith, which vigorously remains steadfast in good times as well as bad. This spiritual mother defended the affairs of your most peaceful empire, namely, the Apostolic Church of Christ, which through the grace of almighty God is proved never to have erred from the course of apostolic tradition, nor succumbed to the depravities of novel heretics. From the beginning of the Christian faith she has secured by means of the authoritative princes of the Apostles of Christ, with the unimpaired goal remaining in her power, according to the divine promise of our Lord and Savior himself, which was confessed by the prince of the disciples in the holy

49

Gospels, Peter, saying 'Peter, behold, Satan has asked to sift you like wheat, but I have prayed for thee, that thy faith shall not fail, and thou, when thou has been converted, strengthen thy brethren.' Let your tranquil mercy consider that the Lord and Savior of all, whose faith it is, who promised the faith of Peter was not going to fail, admonished him to strengthen his brethren, which the Apostolic Pontiffs, the predecessors of my scanty [Pontificate] have always done, and which has been acknowledged by all."

Here, note that Agatho not only says the faith in the see of Peter did not fail, nor could fail, and hence the Pope cannot, as Pope, settle something against the faith; but even that all his predecessors, one of which is Honorius, always resisted heresies and strengthened the brethren in faith. And further on, after Agatho enumerated the Monothelite heretics, Cyrus, Sergius, Pyrrhus, Paul, Peter and Theodore, he said: "Hence, the holy Church of God must be delivered and freed from the supreme endeavors and errors of such teachers, in order that the evangelical and apostolic rectitude of the Orthodox faith, which was founded on the firm rock of this Blessed Peter, Prince of the Apostles and of the Church, which remains inviolate by his grace and protection from every error, every number of prelates, clergy and people will confess and preach with us." The whole council in the eighth action, and in the 18th approved this epistle, where the Fathers not only said that Agatho spoke, but that St. Peter spoke through Agatho.

Therefore, from these testimonies I argue: If Honorius was a Monothelite heretic, then how could Agatho, disputing in the face of this very heresy, write that none of his predecessors ever erred? And when the other churches were stained by the errors of their Prelates, only the Roman Church remained intact? Then, if the council affirmed that Peter spoke through Agatho, and said: "the Roman Pontiffs always confirmed their brethren in faith, and never succumbed to heresy," with what temerity would the same Council in nearly each action say anathema to the heretic Honorius? Therefore it must be that either the council was falsified; or the epistle of Agatho, or that the council is opposed with itself and with Agatho. Now, noone has ever asserted this last one, not even the heretics; on the second there was never any suspicion; therefore it is necessary to hold the first.

Nilos responds to this last argument, but in vain: "Perchance Agatho was moved, both from the fact that the reasoning of the question demanded, as often happens, that he should so write; and because really that Church had erred from the truth more rarely."

But the reasoning of the question certainly demanded that he would say something on his authority, and on the praises of his predecessors. But would it demand that he would impudently lie?

Would it not also have been a very impudent lie for Agatho to say that all his predecessors always resisted heresy, if Honorius, whom he was speaking about, was contaminated with that heresy? It is not enough to say that the Roman Church erred more rarely in order to maintain that it had truly never erred. But let us listen to the rest. Nilos continues: "Otherwise, if this were true, simply and without exception (that no Roman Pontiff erred), how would that agree with what [Scripture] says; 'All have sinned and we are all guilty; there is not one who does good, not even one?'"

Certainly outstanding reasoning, as if David spoke on faith and not on morals. The Psalmist does not say that there is not one who believes rightly, rather "There is not one who does good," and James says: "For we all have offended in many things." Otherwise, if he meant on faith, it would follow that even Paul, and John and all the Apostles could err, even after the reception of the Holy Spirit.

Nilos continues: "It may be that this is rightly said that when Agatho spoke, he meant that in past times the Roman Church did not err, but not that it would be impossible to err in the future." But Honorius, O good Nilos, was in past times. He preceded Agatho by many years. Moreover, did not Agatho speak on the future, when he said that the faith in the See of Peter *would* never fail?

Lastly, Nilos adds: "Agatho certainly wrote these things before the Sixth Council, for then he was not sufficiently acquainted with the matters on which the Sixth Council treated. It would be no great wonder if that holy council examined matters which one man alone could not sufficiently discern."

But if this is so, then Agatho erred from ignorance. Yet why did the whole council in the 8th and 18th action approve that epistle, as though it were written by St. Peter? Why is this anything else than to say the whole council either approved error, or is clearly opposed to itself? I will pass over the fact that no one better understood the doctrines of Honorius than Agatho, since the matter is made plain by John IV. It was more often examined by Theodore, Martin and other predecessors of Agatho, the successors of Honorius.

Fourthly, it is proved from the epistle of Nicholas I to the Emperor Michael, where Nicholas says on the Roman Pontiffs: "For at no time has even a wicked rumor ever defiled us; and when perverse things are discerned with the wise, do they not dispute them all the more?" But how is this true, if in a public, celebrated and well attended general council, it was so often acclaimed 'anathema to the heretic Honorius'?

Fifthly, it is proved because it is either necessary to say that this council, where it condemns Honorius, was corrupted by rivals, or it is fitting to assert this same council labored under intolerable error and impudence; but this second has never been said even by heretics, therefore the first must be said. Moreover, the council could not

53

condemn Honorius for a heretic without intolerable impudence and error, since it is certain it had no other indication of the "heresy" of Honorius except from his epistles to Sergius, where Honorius forbids one or two operations to be said in Christ. But those epistles very clearly witness that Honorius considered and taught two operations in Christ and he only wished for Sergius to abstain from the use of those words "one", or "two" to remove scandal and pacify contention. Moreover, he cannot be condemned as a heretic when he confessed the matter itself, although he thought the name could be kept silent for a just cause, especially before a definition of the Church. Otherwise, St. Jerome could now be condemned as a heretic because in his epistle to Damasus he sensed it must not be said in God there are three hypostases, the contrary of which the Church later defined, and not only once.

Lastly, it happens that a well-attended Roman Council (which was celebrated by Pope St. Martin I, a Pope and a martyr, before the Sixth Council), took up the case of the Monothelites. Sergius, Cyrus, Pyrrhus and Paulus were condemned by name, but no mention was made of Honorius. This cannot be attributed to human respect, since these bishops were very holy men, and especially St. Martin, who presided over the council. Much less can it be attributed to ignorance or forgetfulness. Who would better know the deeds of their successors? Therefore, if the Roman Council did not condemn Honorius, which had his epistles in its own hand as well as living witnesses of his words and deeds, how credible is it that the Sixth Council would do it from his epistles alone?

What if someone were brought in that could not believe that the Sixth Council would be corrupted; he could look to another solution, which is in Juan de Torquemada.[9] He teaches that the Fathers of the Sixth Council condemned Honorius but from false information, and hence erred in that judgment. Although a legitimate general council could not err in defining dogmas of faith (and the Sixth Council did not), still it could err in questions of fact. Therefore, we can safely say that those Fathers were deceived by false rumors and did not understand the epistles of Honorius, and wrongly enumerated Honorius with the heretics.

You will say: Therefore, you understand the epistles of Honorius better than so many Fathers? I respond: Certainly not me, but by John IV, Martin I, Agatho and Nicholas I, the Supreme Pontiffs, and by the Roman Council gathered under Pope Martin, these epistles were better understood than by the Greeks in the Sixth Council.

Why, therefore, you will ask, did the legates of Agatho not protest when Honorius was condemned? I respond: It would have been done to avoid a greater evil. The legates feared if they would have protested that a definition of right faith would be impeded, and a schism which had endured

---

[9] Dde Ecclesia lib. 2, cap. 93.

55

for sixty years, would not be healed. For in that council many patriarchs were condemned, of Constantinople, Alexandria and Antioch, whose successors would not easily have acquiesced unless also Honorius were condemned, who had been accused together with them. And thus the second argument.

Now I respond to the third: The Fathers of the Seventh Council followed the Sixth, and only repeated what had been read in it. Hence they were deceived from the Sixth Council, which was either corrupted or had condemned Honorius in error.

To the fourth I respond: Adrian, with the Roman Council, did not clearly say that Honorius was a heretic, but only that anathema was said to him by the Orientals, because he had been accused of heresy. There it seems Adrian, on that account, had said Honorius was anathematized by the Oriental bishops, because he knew he was not anathematized by the Western bishops, that is by the Council of St. Martin. Moreover, Adrian added that even in the case of Honorius, the Eastern bishops would not have dared to pass judgment on Honorius unless the Roman See had already given its consent, because he knew the legates of Agatho consented to the condemnation of Honorius, and indeed we say this if the acts of the Sixth Council are to be defended as if they are intact; if we were to say they were corrupted, then the response will be that Adrian was deceived by those corrupted acts of the Sixth Council.

## CH. IV: ON POPE HONORIUS I

You might say: But certainly these Councils believed that the Pope could err. I respond: Those Fathers only believed that the Pope could err as a private man, which is a probable opinion, although the contrary seems more probable to us. That is all that Honorius is accused of, that he fostered heresy in *private letters.*

To the fifth I say: Melchior Cano errs twice in this argument. First, when he says Agatho said anathema to Honorius; it is not discovered in his epistles. But Cano seems to have been deceived by the work *Summa Conciliorum,* for the author of that work added the name of Honorius against the faith of those epistles which are contained whole in the second volume of councils. Next, when he says this epistle of Agatho was written to the Sixth Council. Both epistles were not written to the council, but to the emperor.

To the sixth argument I say: The same men who corrupted the Sixth Council also corrupted the epistle of Leo. If that epistle were to be thought of as some part of the council, it is fashioned with that council. Or else Leo followed the judgment of the legates of Agatho, lest he would disturb a business that was already settled. But we are not held anymore to follow one Leo than so many other Popes, especially in a question of fact, which does not pertain to the faith.

To the seventh argument: I object authors to authors, many to a few, and more ancient to more recent; for in the first place, St. Maximus (who lived in the time of Honorius), in the *Dialogue against Pyrrhus*, as well as Theophanes the Isaurian in his history which Onuphrius and Emanuel Calleca cite in a book (which he wrote for the Latins against the Greeks), always witnesses the fact that Honorius was Catholic. Next, even Photius, a Greek, and hostile to the Roman Church, in a book on the seven councils, where he comes to the Sixth Council, says that those who were condemned were Cyrus, Sergius, Pyrrhus, Paul and Peter, but he says no such thing of Honorius. Likewise, Zonaras, in his life of Constantine IV, relating the names of those condemned in the Sixth Council, omits Honorius, just as Paul the Deacon in the life of the same Constantine IV. Lastly, almost all Latin historians such as Bede, Anastasius the Librarian, Blondus[10] Nauclerus, Sabellicus, Platina and others have it that Honorius was a Catholic and holy Pope.

I have added even Bede, even if Melchior Cano refused. I do not doubt whether he thought the same thing, although in his book *de sex ætatibus*, the name of Honorius crept in among those who were condemned in the Sixth Council. It seems some scribe added the name of Honorius in the book of Bede, for the reason that in the Sixth Council everywhere he is discovered with the names of Cyrus, Sergius etc. That Bede held Honorius for a holy man, even after his death, is clear from book 2 of his *History of the English*

---

[10] Decadis primae, lib. 9.

## CH. IV: ON POPE HONORIUS I

*People*, chapters 17-19, where he speaks often of Honorius as the best of shepherds.[11]

---

[11] Translator's note: As with the case of Liberius, it is important to note that Bellarmine is not infallible even though he was a great theologian and historian. While nearly all theologians at his time argued this based on the work of Cardinal Baronius and others, theologians in the later 18th and 19th centuries judged that Bellarmine's second opinion is more probable, namely that Honorius was condemned but this was by way of concession. When the case was reviewed at Vatican I it was judged that Honorius was condemned for not having done enough to stop heresy. Therefore, while Bellarmine's argument is still possible, since councils can err in points of fact (and we add that he brings many good testimonies that make his case), nevertheless, it has been superseded in the estimation of theologians and Church historians.

# CHAPTER V

*On Seven Other Popes*

HE TWENTY-FOURTH Roman Pontiff who is accused of error is St. Martin I, whom the Centuriators[1] accuse because he taught that forgiveness is not to be given to priests or deacons after their ordination for sins,[2] which seems to be a species of Novatianism.

I respond: Martin did not speak on forgiveness of sins, but on the restitution to their sacred ministries. He wished priests and deacons who grievously sinned to be deposed from their state, and if they should come to their senses and seek forgiveness, they should be absolved from their sins, but never restored to their state, which is what all the Fathers teach.

The twenty-fifth is Pope Gregory III, whom the Centuriators accuse, 1) that in an epistle to St. Boniface, he commanded all of those who had been ordained by anyone apart from those whom the Roman Pontiff had sent to be consecrated again.[3] But this is clearly a lie. Gregory only commanded those that were not ordained by true bishops must be consecrated again.

2) They accuse him, in another epistle to St. Boniface, of permitting a man to marry another

---

[1] Cent. 7, ch. 20.

[2] Epist. Ad Amandum.

[3] Cent. 8, ch. 10, in the life of Gregory III.

woman, if, on account of some disease, his own wife is not well enough to render the marriage debt. Gratian also records this.[4] St. Gregory the Great is also accused of the same error by several, on account of his epistle to Augustine of Canterbury, in which the same words are found.

I respond: In the first place, one must marvel why the Lutherans would hold this for an error, since Luther taught the same thing, as John Cochlæus shows.[5] Next, I say that Gregory did not speak on any sort of imbecility, but on perpetual and natural impotence, through which a woman is unsuitable for marriage. Such marriages, if they were contracted from error, are not reckoned to be marriages and they are dissolved in the judgment of the Church as we see it in the decretals,[6] and the Glossa responds in like manner.[7]

But against this, Gregory seems to judge that the first was a true matrimony, and not dissolved as much as added according to it. He writes that a man ought not to take away the subsidy from the first wife; that is, he ought to still support and sustain her as a wife. Therefore, it could also be said with

---

[4] Canon: Quod proposuisti, 32, quest. 7.

[5] Septicpite, cap. De Matrimonio.

[6] Tit. De frigidis, cap. ex literis. Translator's note: In the event that the reader is confused, the Church teaches that one must have the capacity to engage in marital relations in order to truly have a Sacramental marriage.

[7] In 20. D. can. E libellis.

the same Glossa,[8] that the Pope spoke on each infirmity, but not to concede another spouse as though it were just, but rather less bad. It seems less bad that someone should have one concubine, than that he should consort with many harlots. Or, certainly, the Pontiff fell from ignorance. But we do not deny that it could happen to the Popes when they do not define something as *de fide*, but only declare an opinion to others. Gregory seems to have done this in this citation. Moreover, it must be noted that this opinion was not of Gregory I, but only of this Gregory III, since it is not discovered among the works of St. Gregory, but only in the volumes of councils. There, the Roman Council, on the prohibited degrees in regards to matrimony, is attributed to Gregory I and III, when still really it could not be so unless it originated from Gregory III. Such is clear from names of the emperors who appear in the beginning and end of the council.

The twenty-sixth is Nicholas I, whom several condemn, because he taught that baptism conferred in the name of Christ, without expression of the three persons, was valid.[9] That is contrary not only to the evangelical institution, but even to the decrees of other Popes, namely, of Pelagius and Zachary, who condemned the baptism of those who are only baptized in the name of Christ and not expressly in the name of the Father, and of the Son,

---

[8] In 32 quaest. 7, can. Proposuisti.

[9] As is related de consecr. Dist. 4, can. A quodam Judaeo.

and of the Holy Spirit, and is clear in the same place.[10] Nor can the response be given that in the time of Nicholas, it was still not defined whether baptism was invalid if conferred in the name of Christ, for that was defined in the English Council and confirmed by Pope Zachary who preceded Nicholas.[11]

I respond: Nicholas was not defining a question on faith when he spoke; rather, he only expressed his opinion in passing as a private teacher. For what he intended to teach in that canon was not on the form of baptism, but only on the minister concerning which he had been asked. Therefore, after he responded and defined that baptism was valid, even if given by a Jew or a pagan, which the question was especially about, he added in passing that baptism is valid whether it is given in the name of the three persons or in the name of Christ alone. In this he followed the opinion of Ambrose as he says himself.[12] Still, in my judgment, this opinion is false, but not heretical. There is no certain definition of the Church that is discovered on this affair, and various opinions are discovered among the Fathers.

Now those canons of Pelagius and Zachary also do not obstruct the case. In the first place, Pelagius did not define anything, but in his epistle to

---

[10] Dist. 4, can. Mulsti; and can. In Synodo.

[11] Canon "in Synodo", de consec. Dist. 4.

[12] Sententiam lib. 1, de spiritui sancto, cap. 3.

Gaudentius explains his opinion only as a teacher. Moreover, the canon of Zachary is exceedingly suspect. In the first place, Gratian cites the epistle of Zachary to Boniface, when he places this canon, but such an opinion is not discovered in the epistles of Zachary to Boniface, which are extant in the volumes of councils.

Next, Bede makes no mention of this English council in his history, where he always makes mention of other English councils. Nay more, Bede himself follows the contrary opinion,[13] as he approves the opinion of Ambrose on baptism in the name of Christ. Still, one could not ignore a decree of an English council, if it were real, which Zachary mentions, since he lived in the same time and still outlived Zachary. It does not seem at all believable that he would wish to contradict a council celebrated in his own country and confirmed by the Apostolic See.

Yet, if we admit the authority of this council and Zachary, we can respond twofold. Firstly, with St. Peter Lombard that in this council it was only defined that baptism was not valid without the invocation of the three persons. Still, it was not defined whether the three persons ought to be named explicitly, and hence this cannon is not opposed to the opinion of Ambrose and of Nicholas, who taught that it sufficed to implicitly name the

---

[13] Actor. cap. 10.

three persons in the one name of Christ.[14] St.
Bernard also understood that canon of the council
in this manner[15] as well as Hugh of St. Victor and
all other teachers of that age, who taught, not
withstanding the canon of the English Council, that
baptism in the name of Christ was valid.

It can be said secondly, that the English Council
was not truly and properly approved by the
Apostolic See, and therefore does not make the
matter *de fide.* Zachary certainly praised the English
Council, and cited its decrees for his proposition;
still, he did not properly approve it as Pope and
with the intention of confirming the acts of the
Council. It is one thing for the Pope to confirm the
decrees of Councils in earnest, and another to
commend something that other [Councils]
proposed.

The twenty-seventh Pope is Stephen VI, who
can be joined with the twenty eighth Pope accused
of error, Sergius III. It is certain from Platina and
others, that Stephen invalidated the acts of Pope
Formosus, his predecessor, and commanded those
ordained by him to be ordained again. Hence he
thought that the Sacrament depended upon the
virtue of the minister, which is a manifest error in
faith. For that reason, Pope John IX afterward
invalidated the acts of Stephen VI and approved the
acts of Formosus. But a little afterward, Sergius III

---

[14] 4 dist. 3.

[15] Epistle 340.

again invalidated the acts of Formosus, and hence also of John, and approved the acts of Stephen. Necessarily, one of these Popes was opposed to the others and erred, as the Centuriators diligently observed.[16]

I respond: Stephen VI and Sergius III erred in a question of fact, not of law, and gave a bad example, not false doctrine. This is the history. Formosus, the Cardinal bishop of Portus, was deposed by Pope John VIII, and demoted and returned to the lay state, after which he swore that he would never return to the city, or the episcopate. A little after the death of John VIII, his successor, Martin II, absolved Formosus of his careless oath, and restored him to his original dignity. Not long after that, Formosus was created Pope. He lived for five years and died.

Stephen VI succeeded him who, being enkindled with great hatred against Formosus (or else unaware or not believing that he was absolved of his oath by Pope Martin), decreed publicly in a C\council of bishops that Formosus was never a legitimate Pope and therefore, all his acts were invalid. He compelled all those who had received orders from him to be ordained again, just as if they had received nothing. This deed displeased everyone, and therefore three Popes in succession, Roman I, Theodore II and especially John IX, after calling another Episcopal Council, judged that

---

[16] Cent. 9, ch. 10, in the life of Stephen VI, and Cent. 10, ch. 10 in the life of John IX and Sergius III.

## CH. V: ON SEVEN OTHER POPES

Formosus was a true Pope and invalidated the sentence of Stephen VI. Next, Sergius III succeeded him and imitated Stephen VI in all things. The particular question was whether Formosus was a legitimate Pope. We do not deny that in such questions Popes can err, and Stephen and Sergius erred in fact.

But you will object: Stephen and Sergius not only judged that Formosus was not a true Pope, but even the sacred orders which he conferred were not valid; such is a manifest error against faith. Even if Formosus was not a Pope, and always remained deposed and demoted, still, because he was at one time a true bishop, and insofar as the character and power of orders cannot by any means be taken away, it is an error in faith to say that the sacred orders he conferred were not true orders.

I respond: Stephen and Sergius did not publish some decree whereby they determined the orders by a demoted bishop, or the orders that Formosus by name conferred after he had been demoted, must be conferred again; rather, they only *de facto* commanded them to be conferred again. Such a command proceeded not from ignorance or heresy, but from hatred against Formosus. Sigebert remarks in his *Chronicle* for the year 803 that Stephen VI was forcefully opposed by all those who were ordained by Formosus.

The twenty-ninth Pope is John XIII, or as some say, the XIV, whom the Centuriators accuse of a horrendous error and sacrilege, because he began to baptize bells against the institution of Christ, which other heretics frequently use in their objections against us. I wonder why they do not also say that we used to catechize and instruct the bells so that they could ring out the creed! They either condemn the matter itself, or the name "Baptism of Bells." In the matter, clearly they are deceived, or else they are lying, for bells are not really baptized but only blessed and dedicated for divine worship, in the manner that churches, altars, chalices and other sacred vessels are blessed, as is clear from the pontifical where the blessing of bells is contained. Yet no mention is ever made there of baptism, and it is not said: "I baptize you in the name of the Father, and of the Son and of the Holy Spirit." Rather, only prayers to God are found there, just as in all other blessings. If they condemn the name, let them know the name of baptism is not from the Popes, but from common speech; as it is metaphorically accommodated to the blessing of bells because the people see the bells are sprinkled with holy water, and meanwhile names are given to them so that some may be distinguished from others.

The thirtieth Pope who is said to have erred is Sylvester II, whom Martin Polanus relates was a magician and sorcerer, and mangled by the devil in the Church of the Holy Cross at Jerusalem (Santa

Croce). The Centuriators[17] and Tilman Hesh[18] relate this narrative. It is a fact that sorcerers, just as the great part of infidels, worship the devil in place of God.

I respond: These are, without a doubt, fables which are told on the witchcraft and death of Sylvester II. For no author of good faith affirms that for certain, and the tomb of this Pope still exists in the Lateran Basilica, with an inscription placed on it by Pope Sergius IV, a holy man by the agreement of all writers, who was only five years after Sylvester. The inscription praises Sylvester as the best Pope. The occasion of making this story on the witchcraft of this Sylvester was because Sylvester was an expert in geometry and also wrote books on the subject. In that age, however (that is the 900s), which was more unlearned and infelicitous, anyone who devoted himself to mathematics or philosophy was reckoned commonly to be a magician. See Onuphrius in his annotation to Platina.

---

[17] Cent. 10, ch. 10.

[18] De Ecclesia, lib. 1, ch. 9.

# CHAPTER VI

*On Gregory VII*

HE THIRTY-FIRST who is accused of error by our adversaries is Pope Gregory, the seventh of that name. The Centuriators condemn him as a heretic,[1] a wizard, seditious, guilty of simony, an adulterer and the worst, not only of all Popes, but of all men. And for that reason they do not call him Gregory, as is his papal name, nor even Hildebrand, his name in life, but "Hellebrand", which in German means the burning embers of hell.

Theodore Bibliander, in his *Chronicle*, would have it that the same Gregory is the very prince of Gog and Magog, and all other heretics of this time detest no Pontiff more than him. Above all Tilman Hesh clearly lies about the evils he relates concerning Gregory VII contained in his book of monks, Popes and their flatterers.[2] Still neither Tilman nor the Centuriators advance any witness apart from one: the testimony of a Cardinal Benno who lived in that time and left behind a written life of Gregory VII.

Reading the book of this Benno, and discovering it to be full of the most impudent lies, I am persuaded of one of two possibilities: either Benno never wrote any such book in that time and

---

[1] Cent. 11, ch. 10

[2] De Ecclesia, lib. 1 ch. 9.

instead some Lutheran is really the author of this book, who published it under the name of Benno; or certainly that Benno did not so much write a life of Gregory VII, as under the name of Gregory, because he wished to depict what the worst Pontiff would do, in the manner in which Xenophon wrote a life of King Cyrus of Persia, not so much to relate what Cyrus did, as much as what the greatest ruler ought to do.

At any rate one must not put any trust in this work of Benno, and that is clear from the contrary works published on the matter of all other authors who lived at that time, in whom one must place greater trust. Both because they are many and he is only one, but also because Benno was created a cardinal by the antipope Clement III, whom the Holy Roman Emperor set up in hatred of Gregory,[3] not by the true Pope as Bibliander falsely relates in his *Chronicle,*[4] where he falsely depicts Benno as an intimate of Gregory. Since he was the cardinal of an antipope, he could not speak well on the true Pope. Moreover, these other authors were of a neutral party confined by some benefice and therefore judged more correctly. That what the rest write is contrary to the things which Benno wrote, can be easily proven.

There are four claims to which everything that Benno writes can be reduced. 1) That Gregory VII

---

[3] Onuphrius, de Pontificibus.

[4] Tabul. 13.

seized the pontificate by military force without either the vote of any Cardinal or a consensus of the clergy and people. But St. Anselm, the bishop of Lugo (who lived at that time), wrote a letter to Wilbert, a man in schism with the antipope Clement III, saying: "That I might speak on our Father, Blessed Gregory, what St. Cyprian wrote about Cornelius: He was made a bishop by the judgment of God and Christ, by nearly all the clergy, and, that I might speak more truly, absolutely by the acclamation of all, from the suffrage of the people who were then present, to the gathering of the elder priests and good men, since it happened that no man before him, since the place of Alexander, that is, the place of Peter, and the step of the sacerdotal chair was vacant, etc." The Abbot of Ursberg relates this epistle in his *Chronicle*, and adds that this Anselm was a very learned and holy man, and was glorified with miracles in life and after death.

The form of election of this Pope is extant in Platina, in these words: "We, cardinals of the Holy Roman Church, clergy, acolytes, subdeacons, priests, with bishops, abbots and many other ecclesiastics present, as well as laity, elect today, 22 April, in the Basilica of St. Peter in Chains, in the year of our Savior 1078, as the true vicar of Christ, Hildebrand the archdeacon, a man of much doctrine, great piety, prudence, justice, constancy, religion, who is modest, sober and continent, etc." Such a form appears to have been preserved by divine providence to argue against the lies of Benno. Likewise, all other authors write the same, whom we will cite below.

2) Benno writes that Gregory VII excommunicated Henry IV even though he was innocent (as the Centuriators make bold to assert).[5] But Stephen, the bishop of Halberstadt, a holy and learned man, wrote in that time these words to bishop Walram, as Dodechinus witnesses in his addition to Marianus Scotus, in the year 1090, as well as Trithemius in his *Chronicle*: "Listen to what is true, not shams; listen to what is more steadfast, not jokes; anyone that sells spiritual dignities is a heretic (simoniac); but the Lord Henry, whom they call king, sells episcopates and abbacies. Indeed Constance, Bambergen, Moguntia and many others, for money; Regensburg, Augsburg and Strasburg for a sword; the Abbacy of Fuldens for adultery; for the episcopate of Munster, which is unlawful to say and hear, he sold for foul sodomy. If you were to impudently deny these things, with heaven and earth as a witness, even all those responding from the furnace with a little knowledge shall deduce this: the Lord Henry is a heretic. For such unlawful evils he was excommunicated by the Apostolic See; he can exercise no power over us, because we are Catholic."

Marianus Scotus, who lived in the time of Henry IV says: "Catholic men, seeing and hearing

---

[5] Cent. 11, cap. 6, colum 264.

73

these crimes, as well as wicked and unheard of
matters like unto them that were done by King
Henry, were constituted with zeal in the Church,
being zealous, like the prophet Elijah, for the house
of Israel. After messages had been directed to Rome
to Alexander the bishop of the Apostolic See, they
bemoaned by letters, as by a groan and affliction of
the living voice, these and other deeds which were
a great many that were said and done by the insane
heretical simoniacs, having King Henry as their
author and patron."[6]

Likewise, Dedechinus, the continuator of
Marianus, in the year 1106 says: "Henry was a
perverse man and it is manifestly certain that he
was cast out from the Church by a just judgment;
for he sold all spiritual things." The same author in
the year 1090 and 1093 relates many crimes of
Henry IV. Also, St. Anselm of Canterbury wrote an
epistle at the same time to Walram, which preceded
his book on unleavened bread, where he calls
Henry the successor of Nero, Domitian and
Diocletian. Next, Lambert of Schaffnaburg relates
not a few crimes of Henry, as well as the Abbot of
Ursberg,[7] Albert Kranz,[8] Joannes Aventinus,[9] to
which authors the Centuriators usually attribute
much. But what does Calvin confess on the matter?

---

[6] Chronicle for the year 1125.

[7] In Chronico.

[8] Metropolis, lib. 5 et Saxoniae lib. 5.

[9] Annalium Boiorum, lib. 5.

He writes thus: "The Emperor Henry, the Fourth of that name, was a capricious and bold man, of no counsel, but great boldness and dissolute life. He had the episcopates of the whole of Germany in his halls, some for sale, others abandoned for plunder."[10]

3) Benno writes that Pope Gregory was a Berengarian heretic; that is, he did not believe for certain that the body of Christ was present in the Eucharist. But certainly nothing less true can be said about this Pope. For (that I might omit the fact that he is called a saint by all writers, that Leo IX and Nicholas II, who condemned Berengarius, always communicated with him, that no approved author, not even Sigebert who had little love for him, has dared to advance such a thing) Gregory himself, while presiding at the Council of Turin as a legate of the Pope condemned the same Berengarius. Guitmundus writes the following: "The Church herself soon condemned the fabrications which had arisen from Berengarius through Pope Leo. Thereupon, he convicted him in the Council of Turin, through the one who is now our blessed Pope Gregory when he was an archdeacon of the same Roman See. Moreover, as it seemed Berengarius himself was corrected, he [Gregory] mercifully received his hands in the Sacrament. When Berengarius later returned to his

---

[10] Instit. Lib. 4, ch. 11, § 13.

vomit, Pope Nicholas of holy memory again refuted him in the general council at Rome."[11]

But lest they might say that Gregory, when he was an archdeacon, was Catholic, but then a heretic when he was made Pope, let Thomas the Waldensian be read where he relates word for word the opinion of this seventh Pope Gregory, which he imposed in the Roman Council against Berengarius in the sixth year of his pontificate, from which it will appear most clearly that Benno is lying.[12]

4) Benno writes that Gregory was a most wicked man, a simoniac, a magician, an adulterer, a murderer, that he covered up all his crimes; and he relates certain histories of which there is not a vestige extant in good authors, and still Illyricus and Tilman pass them off as oracles from heaven.

Nearly every other author who lived in that time, and in later ages wrote the contrary. Now, I will advance the Germans alone. Trithemus in his Chronicle, writes on the council of the emperor: "William, the Abbot of Hirsau, was called to this wicked council, he scorned to do so, for indeed he knew that the vicar of Christ was holy and innocent." Otho of Frisia says: "Hildebrand was always constant in ecclesiastical rigor."[13] And in the same work, he says: "The form of the flock became what he taught by word, he showed by example;

---

[11] De Eucharistia, lib. 3.

[12] De Sacramentis, tomo 2, ch. 43.

[13] Histor., lib. 6, ch. 32.

being strong, he did not fear to place himself as a wall for the house of the Lord through all struggles."[14] Again: "The Church, bereaved of such a pastor, who among all priests and Roman Pontiffs, was of outstanding zeal and authority, had no little sorrow."[15] Kranz says: "Henry IV encroached upon the laws of the Church, establishing bishops at will, forsaking the Supreme Pontiff Gregory VII, and he persecuted that holy man."[16]

The Abbot of Ursberg does not seem to have dared to praise Gregory VII too openly, yet still, in three places, he shows his opinion. Firstly, where he reproaches Henry IV in clear words: "In the year of our Lord 1068, King Henry, having used the freedom of adolescence, began to dwell in Saxony alone from all the Empire. He despised princes and oppressed nobles, while raising those of lower rank on high, and devoted himself to hunting, soft living, and other exercises of this sort, more than to justice which needed to be done, as he has been condemned. He married daughters of nobles to anyone of obscure birth; he set up private guards, not trusting the powerful very much.... This last end, ruin and lot of Henry was to be known as the fourth Roman emperor under that name by his own; but by Catholics, that is, by everyone united to Blessed Peter and his successors, preserving trust

---

[14] Ibid, ch. 34.

[15] Ibid, ch. 36.

[16] In Metropoli, lib. 5, c. 20.

and obedience to Christian law, he was called the chief of pirates, together with heresiarch, apostate and persecutor more of souls than of bodies." There, while he teaches that Henry sunk from adolescence into tyranny, he shows that the judgment of Gregory against the same king was just.

Next, below that, when he cited the words of the assembly against Gregory, and then the defense of St. Anselm for the same Gregory, the Abbot so adds: "bishop Anselm wrote these things exceedingly contrary to his earlier opinion, a man clearly erudite in letters, with a keen intellect, particular eloquence, and what is best of all, he was most noted in the fear of God and holy conversation, to the point that both in life and after death, he is glorified by the relation of miracles." Certainly, it is no wonder if he who places those that praised Gregory before the condemners, also, seems to tacitly praise Gregory.

Later, he speaks about the successor of Gregory VII: "Desiderius, a Roman cardinal, abbot of Cassino, and true servant of Christ, although he struggled much in heart together with his body. But laboring with great infirmity, he was brought forth to this supreme apex and he obtained by prayers, that he would be taken from this life in a few days." Who could question that this Desiderius, if he was a true servant of Christ, would never have approved the cause of Gregory, unless he recognized it was most just?

Nauclerus, in his *Chronicle*, says: "Gregory was a religious man, fearing God, a lover of equity and justice, constant in difficulties, who, on account of God, did not fear to complete anything in those matters which pertain to justice."[17]

Marianus Scotus, a monk of Fulda, who lived in the time of Gregory VII, says: "Having heard the just complaints and cries of Catholics against Henry, as well as the barbarity of his crimes, burning with the zeal of God, Gregory then pronounced excommunication on the aforesaid king, particularly due to simony. What he did greatly pleased many Catholic men, although the simoniacs and flatterers of the king were greatly displeased."[18]

Dodechinus the abbot, the continuator of Marianus, adds for the year 1085: "Urban himself confirmed the writings and declarations of the venerable Pope Gregory against the schismatics." And, in the year 1090, names Gregory "Pope of blessed memory".

Lambert Schaffnaburg, who lived in the same time, in his history of German affairs, says: "The constancy of Hildebrand, his spirit unconquered against avarice, excluded all arguments of human fallacy... The signs and wonders that were done more frequently by the prayers of Pope Gregory and his most fervent zeal for God and ecclesiastical

---

[17] Chron., gener. 37.

[18] In Chronico, anni MLXXV

laws sufficiently fortified him against the poison tongues of his detractors."

Likewise, he relates the death of William, bishop of Utrecht, who opposed Gregory together with Benno: "Immediately seized by a grave illness, he uttered miserable cries in the presence of all; then, by a just judgment of God, lost the present as well as eternal life, because he had offered to the king his devoted labor for all things which he had so criminally done, and also in the hope of his favor, knowing the grave contumelies against the most holy Roman Pontiff, a man of apostolic virtues, even calling for penalties against him when he was innocent."

Next, he says in the same place: "The Pope, after he celebrated a solemn Mass, advanced upon the king with the Lord's body in his hand and clearly declared: 'For too long I have been accused by you and your flatterers that I took possession of the Apostolic See by simony and that I have stained my life with other crimes. Therefore, I am cutting short such satisfaction, that I shall take away every scruple from every scandal; I ask God that, by his judgment, he might absolve me from the suspicion of the adjacent crime, if innocent, or that I might be killed immediately if guilty.' Then he took up part of the Lord's body and ate. This being freely done, since the people rejoiced in the innocence of the Pope and applauded him in praises of God for a considerable time, he turned to the king and said: 'Please, do what you have seen me do.' The king, after procuring a postponement, refused to cleanse himself or his injustices in this manner; for after he went back to his own, he returned to his normal character and would not rest until he had expelled St. Gregory from the city and substituted Gilbert of Ravenna in his place."

John Aventinus remains from the Germans, who wrote in our century. Although he writes many things on Gregory from some author without a name, and for that reason is without authority, still he was occasionally overcome by truth. He condemned Henry and praises Gregory: "Henry burned with the infamies of sexual affairs, lovers, unchastity and adultery, which even his friends do not deny."[19] And in the same place: "Gregory emerges as a most holy steadfast man. Paul Bernrietensis, who recounts his life in two books, and his remaining shrewd champions, advance his side."

Thus we have the innocence of Gregory proven three-fold: by the testimony of writers, the testimony of dying adversaries, and the testimony of God, when invoked by the Pontiff. Only one calumny remains, namely, that of Sigebert in his *Chronicle*, where he writes that Gregory VII thought that, should priests who had concubines wish to carry out sacred functions, they could not really consecrate, and for that reason, forbade Christians to communicate with priests who had concubines.

---

[19] Annalium Boiorum, lib 5, pag. 563.

I respond: Sigebert was among the secretaries
of Henry IV, as Trithemius relates in his *Catalogue
of Writers*, and therefore he interpreted the interdict
of Gregory in a perverse manner. Moreover, what
Gregory commanded is far better and more
faithfully related by St. Anselm, who is older and
holier than Sigebert. He says: "On the priests who
are publicly reproved and show themselves to God
cursed by carnal relations, it must altogether be
feared that apostolic providence constituted an
ecclesiastical and just rigor, without a doubt, it is by
no means fitting that there one might reverently
assist where they, making a stench with impudent
lust, scorn the prohibition of God and the saints,
and forsake sacred altars; nay more, they do not
merely forsake them, but they have foully defiled
them in the same measure. Not in the way in which
someone will scorn those things which he treats,
but rather he thinks those treating them so must be
cursed just like those who do not reverence the
presence of God and angels, or are repulsed by the
detestation of men; they must cease to contaminate
sacred things."[20] He correctly explained the decree
of Gregory that was published in his own time.

Now, it is fitting to ascribe a catalogue of those
authors who wrote honorably about Gregory VII.
First, Leo Hostiensis wrote in the age of Gregory
himself (around the year 1080) many things on his
sanctity in which there are also heavenly

---

[20] Epist. 8 ad Gulielmum Abbatem.

revelations and visions of approved servants of God.[21] In the same time period, Marianus Scotus wrote on Gregory as a holy Pope from the year 1075 even to the year 1083.[22] Likewise Lambert Schaffnaburg,[23] and St. Anselm of Canterbury.[24] St. Anselm of Lucca in his epistle to Guibert and Stephen Halberstatensis in his epistle to Walramus found in Dodechinus, in an addition to Marianus Scotus. Bernard Corbeiensis[25] which Trithemius witnesses in his *Catalogue of Writers*, as well as Guitmundus.[26] Next, Paul Berniensis, and Gerochus Reichersperg, who wrote on behalf of Gregory and for that reason suffered exile, as John Aventinus witnesses.[27] These, therefore, constitute ten holy and learned writers who defended Gregory while he was alive. The only one who accuses him from these writers is the pseudo-cardinal Benno.

Next, around the year 1100 we have Sigebert, in his *Chronicle*. We already noted how he favored the Emperor Henry IV; still, he never dared to ascribe any crime to Gregory of the sort which Benno and the Centuriators relate; he only attributed to him inconsiderate zeal, and error concerning the

---

21   Historiae Cassinensis, lib. 3.

22   Lib.3 Chronici.

23   *Historia Germanica*, near the end.

24   Epist. 8 et initio libri de azyma.

25   In Apologia pro Gregorio.

26   De Sacramento Eucharistiae, lib. 1&3.

27   Annal. Boiorum., lib. 5.

ministers of the Sacrament, about which Anselm sufficiently exculpates him. Next, the same Sigebert, in the same place, is not silent that Anselm of Lucca wrote for Gregory, and God showed the sanctity of this Anselm by signs and wonders, which certainly pertains to the great praise of Gregory. Not long after, Gratian, in the year 1150, referred to the decree of Gregory.[28] Otho of Frisia, outstanding for his race, erudition and most noble in integrity of life, wrote for our Gregory.[29] Likewise, William of Tyre around the year 1180[30] and Gottfried Viterbiensis.[31]

Conrad, the Abbot of Ursberg in his Chronicle around the year 1200, although he does not clearly praise Gregory, does not reproach him either but he praises him (as we said above) more secretly in many ways, but does not condemn him. In the same time Dodechinus, in an addition to Marianus Scotus, openly praises Gregory, and reproaches Henry. Vincentius, around the year 1250, witnessed that Gregory VII was famous for miracles and the gift of prophecy. St. Thomas cites the same man with honor.[32] Martin Polanus, around the year 1300,

---

[28] 15 quest., 6, canon Nos Sanctorum.

[29] Hist., lib. 6.

[30] De bello sacro, capite 13.

[31] Chronicus universalis, parte 17.

[32] Vincentius, Speculum Historiale, lib. 25, cap. 44.; 2.2. quaest. 12, art. 2.

in the life of the same Gregory. And John Villanus,[33] Blondus around the year 1400,[34] Matthew Palmerius in his *Chronicle* and Thomas the Waldensian.[35] St. Antoninus around the year 1450,[36] Platina, in the life of Gregory, as well as Aeneas Sylvius (Pope Pius II) in the compendium of Blondus. John Trithemius, around the year 1500 in his *Chronicle.* John Nauclerus in his *Chronicle,* Albert Kranz[37] and Sabellicus[38] as well as Volaterranus.[39] They all clearly describe him as a holy man. These are thirty-two authors, whom we oppose to the one witness of Benno, so as to blunt the impudence of the Centuriators and Tilman and certainly to refute the lie of Tilman, who made bold to write that the "crimes" of Gregory VII were brought to light by Monks and flatterers of the Pope, when we have shown the contrary: that Gregory was praised by all.

---

[33] Hist. Florentinae, lib. 4, cap. 21.

[34] Decade 2, lib 3.

[35] Tomo 2, cap. 43.

[36] Secunda Parte Summae Historialis, tit. 16, cap. 1 § 21

[37] Metropolis, lib. 5

[38] Enneade 9, lib. 3

[39] Anthropologiae lib. 22; res gestas Gregorii.

# CHAPTER VII

*On the Remaining Popes to Whom Error in Faith is
Falsely Attributed*

HE THIRTY-SECOND is Alexander III. In the
chapter *Cum esses* (on wills), he says it is
foreign to divine law and the custom of the
Church that more than three witnesses would be
required for wills, and in the same place he
commands under penalty of excommunication that
no one may rescind a will made with three
witnesses. But the contrary is in practice
throughout the whole Christian world; nor are wills
held as ratified unless seven witnesses were applied.
The same Pope Alexander, in the chapter *Licet*, on a
spouse of two people, says that certain predecessors
judged that Matrimony contracted through words
in person, but still not consummated, could be
invalidated through another matrimony; but he
thought the contrary. From which it follows that
either Alexander or his predecessors erred.

I respond: To the first with the Gloss of
Canonists; Alexander did not publish that law
except for men subject to himself in temporal as
well as spiritual affairs; and hence that canon does
not disparage civil laws, nor the practice of the
remaining Christian world. Or if he passed down a
law for all Christians, it ought to only be
understood for pious reasons, concerning which the
Church judges; that is, the Pontiff wished that wills,
not all, but only those which make either the

Church or a local pious person their heir, that they should be valid even if it were made with only three witnesses applied. To the second, I say that neither Alexander nor his predecessors defined anything, but only expressed what they thought.

The thirty-third is Celestine III, whom Alphonsus de Castro asserts could not be excused from heresy in any way, because he taught matrimony could be so dissolved by heresy and that it would be lawful for one to enter into another marriage when his prior spouse had fallen into heresy.[1] Even if this decree of Celestine were not extant, still it was formerly in ancient decretals, in the chapter *Laudabilem*, on the conversion of infidels, which is the decree Alphonsus says that he saw. Moreover, that this teaching of Celestine is heretical is clear, because Innocent III taught the contrary on divorce,[2] and the Council of Trent also defined the same thing.[3]

I respond: Neither Celestine nor Innocent stated anything certain on the matter; but each responded with what seemed more probable to them. That is manifestly gathered from the words of Innocent who, when he says his predecessor thought otherwise, shows in his opinion that the whole matter was still being thought out. On the other hand, Alphonsus says the epistle of Celestine was at

---

[1] De Haeresibus, lib 1 cap. 4

[2] Cap. Quanto.

[3] Sess. 24, can 5.

one time among the epistles in the decretals. While certainly that is true, it cannot thence be gathered that a plainly apostolic decree was made by Celestine, or even one *ex cathedra*; since it is certain that there are many epistles in the decretals which do not make any matter *de fide*, but only declare to us the opinions of the Pontiff on some affair.

The thirty-fourth is Innocent III, who in the chapter, *Per venerabilem*, concerning who might be legitimate sons, teaches the old law was not yet plainly abrogated: "Clearly, since Deuteronomy means the second law, it is proved from the force of the word, that what is discerned there ought to be observed in the New Testament." But this decree of Innocent is opposed to a decree of St. Paul in Acts XV.

I respond: Innocent, in that place, did not wish to say that Deuteronomy ought to be preserved even today by the letter, but insofar as what was said there was a figure of the New Testament. Therefore, Innocent thought Deuteronomy was called second law, because it contained figuratively pertinent matters to the new law.

The thirty-fifth is Nicholas IV, who in the Chapter *Exiit*, on the meaning of the words *in Sexto*, defined that Christ in word and example taught perfect poverty which consists in the abdication of all things, with no ownership being left to himself, neither in particular nor in common, and hence such poverty is holy and meritorious. Yet John XXII taught that this is false and heretical in his

CH. VII: THE REMAINING POPES ACCUSED OF ERROR

*Extravagantes,*[4] on the title of the meaning of the words. For in *Extravagantes,* to the fashioner of the canon, he teaches it is impossible that such poverty whereby someone should swear off all ownership in matters pertaining to the use of consumable things, while only retaining the use; and again in *Extravagantes,* where among several points, he declares it heretical to say that Christ taught such poverty by word and example. Also in *Extravagantes,* under the title of *Quia quorundam,* he teaches the same thing, and more amply drives home the point. Juan Torquemada tries in all things to reconcile these Popes, just as even John himself attempts to show himself to disagree with Nicolas.[5]

But certainly, unless I am greatly deceived, in all things they cannot be reconciled. And therefore, we must observe that John and Nicholas treat three questions. 1) Whether in matters in regard to the use of consumables one can separate use from ownership. 2) Whether poverty, which removes all ownership from itself, being left behind only in use, may be holy and meritorious. 3) Whether Christ taught such poverty by word and example.

Pope John himself responds to the first in the following manner: One cannot separate use from ownership in matters of this sort, for to have

---

[4] Translator's note: Extravagantes refer to papal decrees not contained in certain canonical collections which were obligatory for the Church, but not in the corpus of medieval canon law. There were several by this title.

[5] Summae, lib. 2, cap. 112.

PAPAL ERROR

ownership is to be able to destroy a thing. Hence it
is impossible that one can destroy a thing by use,
such as by eating bread, and not be the master of
that thing. But Nicholas teaches it can be done, and
rightly, for afterward, Clement V clearly taught the
same thing in *Clementina*, "*Exivi de paradiso*," on
the meaning of the words of Nicholas, and the
reasoning is clear. He argues that because one is a
master, he is not able to destroy anything in any
manner; but he can freely destroy a thing after
someone might have wanted it, and even given,
sold, commuted etc. Furthermore, it is certain that
all true religious have the use of the bread which
they eat, and the wine which they drink; still they
cannot give, sell, change or throw them away, etc.
Now, you might say, then Pope John must have
erred. I respond, it is true, but not in the matter
itself; for this question does not pertain to the faith,
as John himself says in *Extravagantes*, because it is
of certain worldly things; and even more, there are
different opinions of teachers on this matter.

On the second question, Nicholas thought that
poverty is holy and meritorious; John denied it.
Furthermore, on each point Nicholas thinks better,
yet Nicholas neither defined this as though it were
an article of faith, nor did John directly oppose it.
For John, in those matters discussed in
*Extravagantes*, to the fashioner of the canons, only
intends to renounce the mastery of those things
which are given to Franciscans, and, as Nicholas

90

asserted, these things were the Roman Pontiffs'; moreover, John could renounce a law of this sort.

On the third question (which is the most serious of all and pertains to faith), Nicholas and John do not disagree. For Nicholas says that at some time Christ taught that most perfect poverty by word and example: moreover, at some time he showed poverty was less rigid by example, just as the common father and teacher of all. Furthermore, John defined it heretical to assert that Christ had nothing of his own here on earth, neither in particular nor in common. These two propositions are not opposed to each other. Nicholas does not deny Christ at some time had something of his own at least in common; rather he denies that Christ always led such a life. John also does not deny that Christ at some time had nothing of his own, neither in particular nor in common, but denies that Christ always led such a life.

That Christ taught each by word and example is proved; for he taught poverty by every means in Matthew X, when he says: "Do not possess gold, nor silver, nor money in your belts, nor a hat nor two tunics, nor shoes or a staff." Neither relates whether these words sound like a precept, or a counsel, and whether they might be expressed otherwise than on abdication of all ownership. For it is enough to preserve the opinion of Nicholas, what this doctrine of Christ might be, and what this sense is not opposed to, as really it is not opposed. Although Christ added: "The laborer is worth his

91

wage," he obligated the people to sustain preachers, and hence conceded to preachers that they might rightly furnish sustenance from the people. Still, he did not oblige those preachers that they should furnish something as though it were due, as is clear from Paul in 1 Corinth. IX, but he permitted them to live on their own labors, even to receive just as a gift without any usurpation of ownership, what is due to them from justice. It happens that in this sense, St. Francis received these words and the institutions; God approved this man with many miracles, as well as the common consensus of the universal Church.

The Lord also shows the same thing in this very example, as is clear from Matthew 8. "The Son of Man does not have a place where he might recline his head," as well as that of Luke 8: "Women followed him, who ministered to him from their resources." For then the Lord lived on the almsgiving of others with the Apostles without a blemish.

The Lord also taught another type of life by his example, which is clear from John 13, where we read that he had places from which he lived in common with his disciples; nor is there a doubt whether they had ownership of certain monies, at least in common, seeing that they had been accustomed to distribute alms, as is clear from the same place. The faithful who were in Jerusalem later imitated such a life,[6] just as nearly all orders of religious. For with the exception of the Franciscans, all have, at least in common, ownership of moveable things.

The thirty-sixth is Pope John XXII, who is condemned by many, and especially by William of Ockham[7] and by Adrian,[8] because he had taught that the souls of the blessed were not going to see God before the resurrection. Erasmus himself affirms this with an addition.[9] He says: "In such an error it appears was Pope John, the twenty-second of that name, being compelled by works of the theologians of Paris to recant in the presence of Philip the king of the French, not without embarrassment. John Gerson says this in his sermon on Easter."

Calvin adds that the same Pope John taught that souls are mortal. "But if they would have the privilege which they claim to be confirmed, they must expunge from their list of pontiffs John XXII who publicly asserted that the soul is mortal and perishes with the body until the day of resurrection. And so, that you would observe that the whole See with its chief props then altogether fell, none of the Cardinals opposed his madness, only the Faculty of Paris urged the king to insist on a recantation. The

---

[6] Acts 4:32-36.

[7] Opus 93, dierum.

[8] Quaestio de Confirmatione.

[9] Prefatione ad li. 5 Irenaei.

king forbade his subjects from communion [with him], unless he would immediately recant; he published an interdict in the usual way by a herald. Thus necessitated, John abjured his error." Yet Calvin does not prove from any source, but placed in the margin: "John Gerson, who then lived, was the witness."[10]

I respond: first, to Adrian. John, at that time, really thought that souls would not see God unless it were after the resurrection: others so reckoned when still it was lawful without danger of heresy, since still no definition of the Church had gone before him. John, moreover, wished to define the question, but while still preparing and in consultations, died, as Benedict XII, his successor, witnessed in *Extravagantes* which begins: *Benedictus Deus*; the whole of which Alphonsus a Castro relates.[11]

Furthermore, John Villanus relates that Pope John, before his death, partly declared and even partly recanted his opinion.[12] First, it is on good evidence that he never had it in his mind, although he had spoken on this matter, to define the question, rather only to treat it so as to discover the truth. Next, he added that John already thought the opinion was the more probable that asserts the souls of the blessed enjoy the divine vision even

---

[10] Institut. Lib 4 cap. 7, §28.

[11] Contra Haeres., liber 3 in verbo Beatitudo.

[12] Histor. lib. 11 Capite 19.

before the day of judgment, and he embraced this opinion, unless at some time the Church would have defined otherwise, and he subjected all his teachings freely to its definition. This retraction simply teaches that the mind of Pope John XXII was always good and Catholic.

To Calvin I say, he most impudently tells five lies in but a few words. First, John Gerson did not live at the same time as John XXII. It is certain from John Villanus[13] and all other historians that John XXII died in the year 1334, while Gerson was born in 1363.[14] Therefore, Gerson was not yet born when Pope John died.

The second lie is that Gerson might have said Pope John denied the immortality of the soul. For Gerson says nothing on the errors of John, except in a sermon on Easter, which is held in volume 4, which alone is cited by all against the error of John. There, moreover, Gerson says: "He did this, to the thief, who seems not yet to have fulfilled the penance for all his sins, yet was beatified and saw God face to face at that proper hour, just as the saints in Paradise. For that reason the falsity of the doctrine of Pope John XXII on that point appears." He neither expresses more what such a doctrine was, but when he said: "There appears the falsity of the doctrine of Pope John," the very reason that the thief crucified with Christ soon after death saw

---

[13] Lib. 11, ch. 19.

[14] Trithemius, de viris illustribus.

God, manifestly shows Pope John erred in this, because he believed the souls of the saints do not see God immediately after death. Yet, neither Gerson nor anyone else who wrote before Calvin, not even William of Ockham, a most hostile enemy of that Pope, asserts that John XXII denied the immortality of the soul.

But I see why Calvin devised such a dreadful lie, because the error of Pope John on the vision of God is not an error for Calvin, but rather a doctrine. For he says only Christ is in heaven; the rest of the saints await in a type of hall even to the end of the world.[15] He adds: "The saints after death are still joined together with us. But if they have faith, therefore they do not see God."[16] Therefore, because Calvin saw what others condemned in Pope John, he could not condemn him; still, he refused to pass over the occasion to accuse a Pope, so he fled to his teacher, the father of lies, and from him changed the whole affair into a characteristic calumny.

The third lie is that no cardinal opposed the teaching of John. This is clearly false, because neither Gerson nor any other says this, and because many thought the contrary, as was clear from the definition which was made by Pope Benedict XII after the death of John from the consensus of all Cardinals which is clear in the epistle of Benedict. Nor was there a reason why these, who thought the

---

[15] Institut. lib 3, cap. 20.

[16] Ibid, §24.

contrary, should fear to oppose John while he was living. Benedict XII, in his *Extravagantes*, asserts that Pope John severely commanded the cardinals and others, all teachers, that they should give their true opinion so that the truth would be discovered. Next, John Villanus, who did live at that time, writes that the greater part of the cardinals opposed the opinion of Pope John while he lived.[17]

The fourth lie of Calvin is that the king of France forbade his subjects communion with John. The fact that King Philip of France believed the Parisian Theologians more than John as a private teacher on that question, is witnessed by Gerson in the cited place; but how, on that account, he would have excommunicated the Pope, no one tells, nor is it believable that a Christian king at that time would have dared to do such a thing.

The fifth lie is that the Pope abjured his error. This, also, neither Gerson writes, nor any other nor ought the Pope abjure error, when he never fell into error. He retracted his opinion the day before he died, but by the advice of those close to him, not at the command of the king. [18] Nor is it true that John was compelled to repent, and it is much less true that it happened in the presence of King Philip.

The thirty-seventh is John XXIII (anti-pope), who at the Council of Constance, sess. 11, is

---

[17] Histoiria, lib. 10, cap. ult.

[18] cf. John Villanus, lib. 11 cap. 19, wherein the calumnies of Erasmus may also be detected.

accused of a very pernicious heresy; for it is said that he denied the future life, and resurrection of the body. I respond: John XXIII was not a Pope, and it is certain and undoubted, hence it is not necessary to defend him at all. There were in those times three men that claimed to be Pope, Gregory XII, Benedict XIII, and John XXIII. It could not easily be determined who among them was the true and legitimate Pope, since none of them lacked very learned men as patrons. I add in addition that it is very probable and nearly certain that the error is falsely attributed to this anti-pope John. For in the first place when in that session of the council the articles that he objected to were enumerated, they first placed 53 articles, which all pertain to custom, and all these were confirmed by certain witnesses. Next, others are advanced without certain witnesses, and the second to last of these is the one on which we are now arguing.

Therefore, this point was not proven, except by common rumor, which, because people saw John was of dissolute life, they began to reckon and even say that he did not believe in the future life or the resurrection of the body. But who does not see that heresy is not truly gathered from bad deeds? How many can be counted who believed rightly and lived a most degenerate life? Next, in sess. 12, the definitive opinion of the council against John also briefly reviewed the reasons for his condemnation and deposition, but no mention is made of error, or of heresy. Certainly the argument is evidence that it cannot be proven that this "Pope John" was an object of heresy. For if it could have been proved, it ought to have been reviewed in the first place among the reasons of condemnation, since there is no more just cause of judging a Pope than the note of heresy; nay more, there is no other reason why a Pontiff can justly be judged.

The thirty-eighth Pope is Benedict XIII, whom the Council of Constance condemns in the name of heresy.[19] But this Benedict was not a legitimate Pope, since he succeeded Clement VII, who had invaded the papal seat while Urban VI was still alive, but still he was not truly a heretic. The only thing objected against him is that he did not believe a council had greater power than the Supreme Pontiff, in which affair Benedict did not err at all.

The thirty-ninth is Eugene IV, whose pontificate was abrogated by the Council of Basel,[20] because he had fallen into heresy. But he also did not err in any truth. Wherefore, the Council of Lausana continued his earlier acts and Nicholas V, the successor of Eugene, was venerated as a true Pope, as can be recognized from the letter of the same Nicholas, which is usually attached to the Council of Basel in the volumes of councils.

The fortieth Pope to be accused of error is Innocent VIII, who seems to have sinned because he permitted the Norwegians to celebrate the sacrifice

---

[19] Sess. 37.

[20] Sess. 34.

without wine, as Raphael Volateranus relates.[21] But this can be answered easily. For in the first place he did not publish a decree wherein he declares something for the universal Church, namely that it is lawful to offer the sacrifice of the Mass without wine. Therefore, if he erred, he erred in fact, not in doctrine. Next, he did not permit another liquor to be confected in place of wine, which would pervert the matter of the Sacrament; he only permitted that they might consecrate the Eucharist only under the species of bread on account of extreme necessity, since in that region wine cannot be preserved, thus it quickly sours. But certainly there is either no error, or certainly the error was not explored. It happens that it is baffling that in that time they did not have the use of wine, or could not preserve it, since in our time it is so frequently used because the heretics do not wish to communicate without it.

# FINIS

---

[21] Geographiae, lib. 7.

www.ingramcontent.com/pod-product-compliance
Lightning Source LLC
LaVergne TN
LVHW021401080426
835508LV00020B/2389